PRAISE

'Ruth is a force of nature and gets stuff done. Her warmth and authenticity shine through.'

Taki Moore, Million Dollar Coach

'Stuck in life? The wonderful Ruth Kudzi will help you figure out your path. This book is a must read for anyone who is ready to step into a bigger, brighter future.'

Noor Hibbert, Success Coach

RETHINK PRESS

First published in Great Britain 2018
by Rethink Press (www.rethinkpress.com)

Cover photographs by Amanda Clarke
(www.amandaclarkephotography.com)

IS *this* IT?

THE SMART WOMAN'S GUIDE TO FINDING **WORK YOU LOVE**

RUTH KUDZI

CONTENTS

To Jessica and Sophia, you are my big why and have made it even more important to do work that I love.

FOREWORD

We all have reasons why we don't take actions and we try to convince ourselves that these are justified. At least in our minds they are, but really they are excuses to stay stuck. Life is too short to be in a job that you don't enjoy or to feel anything less than great about life. We only have one shot.

The truth is, you are the only person responsible for changing the way that you work and how you feel. To do this takes courage; courage to go for your dreams and to live your best life - one that you can be proud of.

Reading this book is a powerful step to making that a reality. It is both a wake-up call and cheerleader, spurring you on and giving you both permission and the tools to start making changes today.

Shaa Wasmund MBE,
Sunday Times **best-selling author**

INTRODUCTION

Do you ever ask yourself, 'Is this it?' Does your life feel more 'meh' than marvellous? Do you spend most of your working week with the nagging feeling that you don't want to be doing the same thing for ever? You know that you don't want to continue in your current job for the next ten, fifteen or twenty years, but you aren't sure what to do next? Part of you says that 'good enough' is OK while the other part spends half her life on Google, looking at jobs and wondering…

Maybe you find the idea of a complete change, perhaps teaching yoga on the beach in Spain, appealing but unrealistic. How do people with commitments and responsibilities change careers? Do they even do it at all?

You don't have to stay with a mediocre life or in a job that isn't fulfilling; you can change career, however old you are, and you can live a life that is more congruent with your values.

In this book we'll explore how you can change the way you work, the job you do and the relationships that you have. You'll identify your strengths and passions and get clear on what you want, as well as formulating a plan of how you are going to get there.

Sounds simple? Change is never simple. There will be some work for you to do if you are serious about this: some inner work (yes, we are going to talk about the brain and your mind), and lots of practical things, too. Whether you make a big change or a series of smaller changes, this change is unlikely to happen overnight, but it *will* happen. And I'll be supporting you along the way.

Change is a scary process, and you may not even know how you want to change, but don't worry. Throughout this book you'll find plenty of case studies and examples of people who have changed their lives in many different ways, and they've gained strength from the support of a private Facebook community of women just like you (www.facebook.com/groups/IsthisitRK).

MY STORY

I decided to write this book as I was the woman I described at the start for a long time. I stayed in my last career because I was scared to leave. I lacked the confidence to make the leap. The conditions were OK, I wasn't in danger, I had a nice life, so what did I have to complain about? I did all the rationalisation on a daily basis and listened to the voices (most of them in my head) that said I should be content with my lot.

For me, everything changed when I had my first daughter, and I found that the things I disliked were magnified. Work had taken on a new aspect, as I was now leaving my daughter to do something I didn't love and was in a constant state of stress, doing my best to make it work. This state of affairs gave me the kick up the bum to do what I had been thinking about for years: setting up my own coaching business. Coaching is where my passion and skills lie, and two and a half years in I couldn't be happier with my choice.

I am a qualified business and confidence coach with a strong interest in psychology and how the mind works (I have an MA in Psychology and am studying for another MSc in Positive Psychology). At the age of thirty-eight, I embarked on this, my third career, having originally worked in sales and recruitment before moving to education, where I was a senior leader. I have worked with hundreds of real women who have changed careers, whether by working in new ways or starting up their own businesses, and I'll be sharing many of their stories with you. And to get even more out of the book, please login to my members' site at www.ruthkudzi.com/isthisit using the code 'bookreader'. There you will find bonus videos and activities to help you get clarity on your next steps. You can also join the Facebook community especially for readers of this book at www.facebook. com/groups/isthisitRK.

You may have picked up this book for many reasons. A lot of my clients are mums who want to have a flexible way of working. For others, the catalyst for change may be redundancy, a relationship breakdown, illness, or the fact they aren't able to have children. It doesn't matter why you have decided that the time is right to make a change; it only matters that you have made that decision.

Throughout the book, you will find out how you are probably the biggest blocker to your own happiness. We will look at how you can overcome obstacles, both real and perceived, so that you can have a fulfilling work life which doesn't overtake your home life. The choices are endless, but the first step is a commitment to saying, 'I am worth more than this. I deserve to feel fulfilled and happy.'

Are you ready to make that commitment? You are in exactly the right place.

Let the journey begin.

Ruth

CHAPTER ONE

SETTING THE SCENE

Does this sound familiar? It is Sunday night and you have spent the entire day in a low level of anxiety, which has stopped you unwinding, relaxing and truly enjoying your time off. You don't want to go to work tomorrow, your passion and drive (if you ever had any) seem to have dried up, and you feel like you are just going through the motions on a daily basis. As soon as you start on Monday, you are thinking about Friday. The dread is there every day, not just on a Sunday.

Everything is measured in time. You, along with your friends, call Wednesday 'hump day' because you have made it to half way through the week. Thursday and Friday are the home straight; Tuesday afternoon is the hardest of the week when the chasm between the previous weekend and the next feels immense. You 'love' the gifs and emojis (and feeds) on Instagram that celebrate hump day and talk about 'Friyay'; in fact, you often create your own.

This is not how you imagined life would be.

It isn't that you hate your job; hate is too strong a word. But you do often wonder if this is really what your life is going to be like for the next twenty to thirty years. You may well have done what you thought you 'should': university, a job where you worked hard and built a career, climbed the ladder. From the outside, your life looks pretty good, but in reality you feel like you are on autopilot, going through the motions. Often there is a compound effect: the commute; the lack of flexibility; the fact that you have to be at work at a certain time every day; the office politics – the list can go on and on.

I understand; I was there too. I never hated my job. In fact, what I did was inherently good as I worked as a senior leader in challenging secondary schools, but if anything this made my feelings of dissatisfaction and disillusionment worse. If I was helping children to learn and make progress, surely I had to be fulfilled, but I felt like a fraud. I would plaster on my smile and my management suit and get on with it, day after day, month after month, year after year. Outwardly, I had a good job, my own place, a partner whom I loved, and a decent lifestyle. Inside,

I felt like I was putting on a façade, when really I was feeling pretty empty.

I had fallen into the trap of being stuck in a job, and I thought that this was how it was and how it was going to stay. I didn't see that there could be other options.

Often, we stay where we are in life because we convince ourselves that this is our lot. We have our steady job and good salary which provides us with a golden cage. The trappings of our mortgage, powerful car, expensive gym membership (whether or not we actually go), and the exotic holidays make us feel like birds that can't escape. We never imagined that the things we have worked so hard for would make us feel like this.

As well as feeling trapped, we are scared of change. We have followed the script of 'shoulds', but we aren't where we imagined we would be. Material and physical successes are masking a lack of real fulfilment and happiness. We find that we are living for our holidays, which offer us a temporary escape from our reality.

I love holidays. When I was at university, my friends used to joke with me that I would struggle when I started working full time as I went on so many. And, aside from a few years in recruitment and sales, I spent most of my career in education with thirteen weeks' leave. How could I complain with thirteen weeks to travel and relax? Surely, I was living my dream? Surely, it didn't matter what the other thirty-nine weeks were like?

The countdown to the holidays was in a way worse than the weekly countdown: only three weeks to go, two weeks to go, one week to go. My only motivation was to get to the next weekend, then the next holiday; I was certainly not living in the moment. Often I was about as present as the teenagers I was teaching cash flow statements to.

It was as though I was wishing my life away, and I know I was future tripping. Future tripping is where we spend all of our time focused on what we think is going to happen rather than enjoying where we currently are, and we can all be guilty of this. Our holidays become a holy grail that will save us from feeling overwhelmed and lacking in fulfilment, but often our standards are so high that we come back feeling worse than before.

Have you ever found yourself becoming ill on holiday? Or counting down the number of days left before you have to return to work with dread? Even on holiday, we can find it hard to relax and switch off properly.

Frankly, it is exhausting, and I know I am not the only one who has felt that way. What people put on their screensavers speaks volumes. One of my friends says that every person in her office has their screensaver counting down to when they are going away on holiday. She walks through the open-plan office, and by the time she gets to her desk, she knows exactly when each of her colleagues will be away.

When the main selling point of your job is how much time you have off, you know things aren't quite right. You spend the majority of your time at work, so it is incredibly important to feel good about it.

DITCH THE GUILT

How often do you make yourself feel bad because you aren't happy? Some days, do you wish that you could have a minor accident or ailment which would give you some respite from your job? If you do, feeling guilty won't make it any better. Guilt is a pretty unforgiving emotion; if you only take one thing from this chapter, make it a decision to ditch the guilt. It doesn't matter what other people think, this is about how you feel.

There are some activities to help you overcome any guilt that may be holding you back in the membership area at:
www.ruthkudzi.com/membershiparea

OVERCOMING THE MISMATCH

The mismatch you feel with your job is often not about you; it's due to the fact that you aren't doing what is aligned with your strengths and your values. My client Lynsay, a career and success coach, describes why she made the change.

> I loved the job I did in HR in the beginning, but as I got more and more senior in my role, it felt like it was more about protecting the businesses I worked for instead of the people in them. And it was the people I'd gone into HR for in the first place. I just felt incredibly out of alignment and didn't feel like I had purpose any more in my job. I dreaded going into the office and was tired of travelling all over the country for work and being away from my husband and children.
>
> Years later, my husband quit his job in optics and went back to university to train to be a high school science teacher. I was super proud of him for going after his dreams, but as I became the main earner in our home at this time, it was even more important that I continued in my job to support us financially.
>
> In September 2015, my husband started his first teaching job. When he got home at the end of his first week, I asked him what he thought of his new job. He said he couldn't imagine doing anything else now and couldn't understand why he hadn't done it earlier. He was

so happy, and I was happy for him, but the over-whelming feeling I had was jealousy. He had a job with a purpose that he loved, and he could see every day the difference he was making to the lives of the kids he was teaching.

That was it for me. That was the moment I knew I had to make a change. I promised myself that by the end of the year, I'd have started my own business.

I'd had lots of false starts in trying to have my own business, but in December 2015, with the support of a trusted mentor and my family behind me, I quit my job and started my business. At first, I contracted for larger UK businesses before moving into working with women who were looking to escape the nine to five and start their own businesses on their terms.

I was finally working for myself.

Lynsay Gould, Career and Success Coach

Often when people around us make a change it can have an impact on us. We see how happy and fulfilled we could be. We then have a choice: take the leap as well or continue to do what we are doing and start to resent those close to us. Lynsay is a great example of someone who channelled the envy she felt towards her husband into creating a hugely successful business.

THE IMPORTANCE OF CULTURE

Have you ever felt that your work persona is different to your real persona? It is important to have boundaries when you manage a team, but I remember getting told off by my boss for being friendly with the people I managed. I was told I had to be a certain way which I felt wasn't aligned with my personality and values, so I ignored this instruction. As a result, I am still friends with people who worked for me and with me.

This is an example of how organisational culture can have a huge impact on how we feel. When the culture doesn't match our values, we can find the mismatch extremely challenging. This inevitably impacts on our performance and how we feel. We never read this in the glossy magazines, though, which insist we must climb the ladder and get a better salary, take on responsibility and have more impact, but fail to mention that we'll have far less fun and social support if we do.

Politics is alive and kicking in most UK workspaces and you have to know your place. If you (like me on one occasion) start in a senior position and don't gel with your immediate peers, it can be very isolating. Often friends are one of the only reasons that we stay in our jobs rather than leave. Having a community around us is good for our mental health and happiness (even if we aren't loving the work). Have you ever stayed in a job because of great people and relationships?

I have spoken about values. These are the things that you think are important in life and they guide the way you behave. By identifying your values, you can often understand why you feel the way you do in certain work environments.

For example, integrity is a core value of mine, but I have been in environments where this didn't seem to be important. This had a negative impact on how I felt and how I performed. Values are personal to each of you, and a mismatch between your values and those of your employer can be uncomfortable for you, often meaning that you don't fulfil your potential.

To help you get clarity on your values, there is a useful exercise in the members' area.

THE CURSE OF THE EMAIL

The working landscape has changed. It has now become the norm to expect people to reply to emails sent after 6pm or at the weekend (although in France, sending business emails after 6pm is outlawed). We may feel we have to show at least a pretence of commitment; we believe that we need to be chained to our emails otherwise our employer may think we don't care. Ironically, in this current climate, many people are actually caring less and less about the work they do.

Recently, a client recounted how her boss sends through the information she needs for the Monday morning meeting on a Friday night (after 6pm). The boss's expectation is clear: spend the weekend working on the tasks set out in this email or be unprepared for the meeting. Even though she may wish she could tell her boss to stuff it she has commitments so she puts up and shuts up.

This sort of behaviour is prevalent throughout workplaces in the UK. Emails have seeped into our everyday lives and we find ourselves checking them in our precious free time, so the boundaries between home and work are becoming increasingly blurred. Often emails are nothing more than someone else's to-do list, but that doesn't stop many of us having considerable anxiety about the size of our inbox. I have been guilty of sleeping with my phone, staying awake late into the night answering emails, which naturally had a negative impact on my sleep. And I know I am not the only one who has had emails from colleagues and bosses at 2 or 3am.

Often, we feel pressure to perform and be present. I know I felt I had to answer emails as soon as they came in, even though others had a much more relaxed approach. If you are constantly checking your email inbox, you aren't giving yourself time to relax or switch off properly so are more likely to be suffering from stress. While on holiday last year, I was chatting to a friend who told me she couldn't switch off. The reason? She is on a work WhatsApp group, and every time it pinged, she felt obliged to reply and be involved. Even when I convinced her to leave the group, she still found it hard to switch off mentally, so her holiday was not as relaxing as she'd hoped. Her work had taken over her life, and the feeling of being 'on' the whole time was exhausting.

I am not talking about unbearable working conditions; I am talking about a general feeling of malaise that you get when you work somewhere that doesn't do it for you. You may feel like your talents are being wasted, or perhaps you have been in the same industry for so long that you feel you don't have any talents left, but when you think about leaving, a little voice in your head says, 'But what else can you do?' It is like being in a relationship that you know isn't going anywhere, but because you are comfortable, you haven't got round to leaving... yet.

If you are like I was just a few years ago, wanting to escape endless emails and office politics and wondering if there is more to life, then read on.

THE CATALYST FOR CHANGE

About fifteen years ago, I remember asking a woman I worked with how she was. She was nine years older than me and in a senior position.

'I am here,' she replied. 'I come in every day and I do my job, but I don't really feel anything. Every day merges into one and I feel like I am just going through the motions. Don't become me.'

With the veneer of youth and excitement, I thought, *of course I won't*, but in a matter of years I was in exactly the same position as her, both in my career and mentally. I didn't admit it to myself for a long time, until having children compounded the problem for me. As my priorities changed, it shone a light on the things which I had been tolerating for so long: the lack of flexibility; the politics; the lack of autonomy and control; the mismatch between my values and those of my employer; the fact that I fundamentally disagreed with a lot of what I was having to do. When I faced the truth that I would be leaving my daughter to do something that made me feel so compromised, I knew it was time to change.

Friends and clients have found illness, divorce, infertility, or even a big birthday to have been the catalyst for change. However, it doesn't have to be anything big. Many studies related to stress have shown that the biggest impact of psychological stress comes when we allow the daily hassles to build up. These then increase cortisol levels, which can lead to problems with our immunity and stress-related illness. According to the Health and Safety Executive (www.hse.gov.uk/statistics/causdis/stress), stress-related illness impacts at least 526,000 workers in the UK and accounts for 12.5 million working days lost each year. And, there is evidence that women aged twenty-five to fifty-four are more stressed than their male colleagues. When I was conducting research for this book, I was shocked at these statistics, particularly as I knew that much data is hidden as many women who are suffering from stress fail to report it.

When I was working as a senior leader, my health was pretty dire. I had eczema and red patches on my skin, I would get auras where my vision went blurry and I had to sit down, and I was constantly exhausted. My exercise was sporadic at best, and I often snacked on crisps and chocolate on the way home. I knew that I wasn't healthy, but outwardly I looked OK. I covered up the eczema with expensive face creams and I kept pushing myself as I was convinced that this was normal. This was the price I had to pay for success.

You may be nodding along while reading this, so let me reassure you that it doesn't matter where you are now. You *can* change your reality, and this book will give you the tools to do just that. My life has

21

completely transformed since I made the change, and my clients say the same thing. Indeed, this book is packed with case studies that show you how other women have changed the way they work and the positive impact it has had on the rest of their lives.

'Fine' is not good enough. You deserve your dream life and a job that you love, so my advice to you is to read this book and take the plunge.

MY ESCAPE ROUTE

For many years, I looked like a successful woman. I had racked up an array of qualifications, and after a stint in sales and recruitment, where I helped open offices in New York and Europe, I moved into education. I had felt unfulfilled in recruitment as the culture was focused around money, which didn't tie into my personal values. I wanted to do something different with my life, but even then, at the age of twenty-seven, I felt too old to be making a change. I was classified as a mature entrant into the teaching profession, which is something that makes me smile now.

Moving into education, I climbed up the ranks quickly and spent over a decade working in leadership roles as a consultant, assistant and deputy head. I cared deeply about making a difference and feeling like I had a positive impact on the students.

I also cared about my teams and worked hard to get the best out of them. But, I wasn't happy. I wasn't as fulfilled as I pretended to be. There were still situations where I felt my values were challenged, which left me feeling uncomfortable.

I was a Sunday night bottle-of-red drinker. I used to go to bed as late as possible to put off the inevitable (not a good strategy as then I would wake up tired on Monday morning, compounding the misery). There were many things that I loved about my job, but I knew my heart wasn't in it, and when I looked at the people who were more senior than me, it filled me with fear. They looked tired, disillusioned and unhappy. That wasn't how I wanted to live my life, but I was scared to leave. Was I flaky to have already changed career once only to walk away from something solid just because I didn't love it? Should I count my blessings gratefully and put up and shut up? During this time, I confided in no one bar my husband.

When I had my first daughter, I dallied with the idea of doing something different, and set up a number of ventures. I coached (I racked up 500+ coaching hours before starting my business), set up a blog, set up a business with my husband, and even developed an app. I spent the summer before my daughter's birth volunteering as a coach for head teachers and other senior leaders, and I absolutely loved it. Working with an incredibly experienced ex-head teacher, I could see how my skills were helping others progress and I believed my path to becoming a coach was to become a head teacher first. My role models had all come to coaching from education, so I thought I could do so too.

Unfortunately, I wasn't successful enough to replace my salary (which was always going to be hard when I wasn't charging) and I headed back to work ten months in. But it didn't take me long to realise that my work was no longer compatible with how I wanted to live my life. The hours meant that I was struggling to spend any time with my daughter during the week, and there were politics and situations at work which made me uncomfortable. For example, I soon became fed up with identifying problems that my employers insisted didn't exist, only for the same problems to be highlighted at a later date by external bodies. I had reached my tipping point and I had three options: get a new job elsewhere, stay at home with my daughter, or follow my dreams and set up the business I had always wanted.

I knew that I wanted to have a coaching business but didn't know how it would work. The wife of a work colleague was becoming successful in a similar field, and we had a few chats which gave me the confidence boost I needed. He was one of the few people I worked with whom I felt I could be honest with, and it was inspiring to know his wife had followed her heart and was now successful.

On the day of my daughter's first birthday, I had to be at work by 7am when she was still fast asleep. That evening, I had to attend a meeting which ran on late, and by the time I got home she was once again asleep. I hadn't spent any time with her. I felt like I was a failure as a mum, and the WhatsApp notifications from my husband about our daughter with him and my mum throughout the day only made it worse.

As the next day was my daughter's first day at nursery I asked if I could come into work one hour later than usual, so I could take her. My request was refused, despite the fact I approved similar requests every day for other members of the school staff (in fact, it was part of my job). This for me was the final nail in the coffin and I started seriously considering my options.

I felt that I had made the wrong choice going back to my full-time job after my daughter's birth. Lots of my friends had had more time off with their babies, and I couldn't help but compare myself to them. Were they better mothers? Would Jessica always remember this day and think I didn't love her as much as other mums loved their children?

I cried a lot that day and for the weeks afterwards. On a personal level, I was devastated. I didn't want to be a career woman if it meant I couldn't spend time with my daughter. Everything felt out of balance, which was a sure sign that something had to give.

I knew that I couldn't stay in the same working environment much longer. I had been coaching in my job for years, had done voluntary coaching, and had studied it, so coaching was the natural path for me. It was one of those 'now or never' moments. So a huge thank you to the man who said I couldn't drop my daughter off at nursery on that fateful day. In a funny way, I owe a lot of my success to you.

While plotting my escape route and feeling increasingly disengaged, I found out I was pregnant with baby number two, giving me the perfect time to set up my business. It was on my new boss's second day in his role that I told him I was pregnant and would be going on maternity leave. Ironically, if he had been my boss for longer than that, my decision would have been harder to make. He was a visionary and an absolutely first-class head teacher with values which were aligned with mine, and he was a great support when I resigned.

A DREAM COMES TRUE

My second pregnancy was plagued by morning sickness and I was exhausted by balancing work and home life. However, I had a goal in mind, so I was motivated. I planned out what my business could look like and completed some NLP and coaching qualifications I had started years before. Letting people in my personal network know what I was doing, I started to build up my coaching hours. I knew that I had to take action and put everything into realising my dream.

Three weeks before I had Sophia, my second daughter, I went on maternity leave. There was no relaxing; I used the time to build a website, coach, and find out about the online world. I knew about business, but I didn't know much about the self-development world, and very little about the online world. I hadn't even heard of Marie Forleo, who is seen as one of the leading online coaches and was an early mentor to me through her B-School program; I was a complete newbie.

This was going to get interesting.

For a month after Sophia had been born, I continued to read, do pro bono coaching and work on my business. I hired two coaches and got my husband to help me on the digital side of things. Although I made many mistakes, by the end of August 2016 I had set up my second Facebook group, which was growing rapidly and was creating my first marketing material.

I positioned myself as a career coach for mums. At the beginning, I was coaching with limited childcare so took on a couple of clients here and there, continued to study (completing a postgraduate certificate in coaching), and learnt from online courses and group programmes which I could fit around my children's needs. After six months, I was in a position to resign from my job as my income had matched my monthly salary, so I knew I could make it work.

Since then, my business has gone from strength to strength. In June 2017, I changed my focus to work with women entrepreneurs specifically on business and mindset, using my background in business, psychology and coaching holistically. After years of coaching, I have found that this is what lights me up and I am best at. Having done a lot of work on myself, I was confident in my abilities and was getting great results for my clients.

I celebrated the three-year anniversary of my decision to start up on my own with cake and prosecco. What's more, I celebrated with my two daughters, and I will never miss their birthdays again.

WHAT'S NEXT?

All this nearly didn't happen. I set my business up because I couldn't see an alternative that would make me feel fulfilled and would work for both me and my family. I had a sliver of self-belief at the beginning, but it had to compete with a bunch of insecurities and blocks. I certainly didn't think I would ever be someone who could talk about having a six-figure business.

But I was wrong. In a short space of time, I have built something I am immensely proud of. The reason for my success? I used my skills and experiences and took action every day to be the best version of myself. I still have a lot to learn, and acknowledge I am far from the finished article, but are any of us?

To be the best version of yourself, you don't necessarily need to start up a business. In fact, you don't need to change what you are doing if you don't want to. I won't have you chanting or meditating (unless you want to). My advice is more about finding out who you are and what you want to do moving forward, discovering a way to work that works for you, your situation, your skillset, your ambition and your values.

This book is about understanding that a mediocre work life isn't your only option. You don't have to put up with it. In fact, you don't have to put up with a mediocre life at all. You *can* leave your job, change your job, retrain or start up your own business. Take the plunge and transform 'meh' into 'marvellous'.

I have done it, and I have helped scores of other women to do it, too. Since I started my business, I have more time with my children, I have travelled all over the world, and I have a much better relationship with my husband. I am happier than I have ever been, and healthier, too; I exercise every day, and I no longer have the eczema that I used to suffer with. I sleep better and I drink less. Feeling fulfilled, I am confident in my own skin.

Helping others to have the same feelings of fulfilment and confidence is my purpose in life. I am passionate about letting people know that no one needs to continue in a job that doesn't light them up. We don't need to settle for fine. We can want more and we can have more. The answer to 'Is this it?' is 'No, it isn't.'

You can live the life that you want to live, and that starts off with your work. Work is such a key part of who you are, and when you have it nailed, everything else tends to fall into place. Life is too short to be any-thing other than the best version of you. The old adage that you can do work you love, but not get the financial rewards, or do work that gets the rewards, but isn't fulfilling is outdated. I now earn more than I did in previous jobs where I was ostensibly successful, and many of my clients have left their career jobs and reported the same.

For some of you, this book will help you seek out new ways of working in your traditional role (like my client Kerry who is a partner in a law firm and works from home around her kids' needs). Others may decide to do something completely different, perhaps achieve the passion project that has been their dream for so long, or retrain for a completely new career. This book will act as your roadmap to finding ways of working that suit you.

In my experience, the biggest regrets people have are always the things that they didn't do. The common wish among my clients is that they had made the change earlier. If you had the opportunity to live the life that you truly desired, would you do everything you could to change? Does this sound better than staying where you are? It isn't always easy and there will almost certainly be challenges along the way, but you will have the support of this book, your handy roadmap, to help you.

CHAPTER TWO

WHY NOW?

You may have been feeling disillusioned and unfulfilled for years or just for a few months. It doesn't matter how long you have been feeling like this, the most important thing is that you have now come to the point where you want to change. So what is it about now that led you to this decision?

In this chapter, we are going to look at two women who have been where you are now and see why they made their decisions to change their lives. Their stories illustrate two very different catalysts for change and explain how each woman made things work.

RECOGNISING OPPORTUNITY

Sometimes, a significant event leads us to re-evaluate and make changes; sometimes, change can happen as a result of a series of daily hassles or small events which leave us feeling unfulfilled. Either way, there is always a reason why we eventually decide that something has to give.

My client Liese talks about how redundancy gave her the opportunity to create her own business.

I'm Liese Lord, and until recently I was a global HR director within a US owned multi-national B2B company. I now have my own consultancy business helping organisations create flexible and agile ways of working for all their employees. My mission is to help as many businesses as I can to free themselves from the modern industrial revolution of the 'nine to five at the office', enabling greater choice of where, when and how their employees work, blending work as part of life, and becoming higher performing organisations as a result.

I had been a corporate employee for many years (decades) until I was made redundant from my role in December 2015. I was not your typical HR person as I like to challenge the norm – I encourage business leaders to stretch themselves and think differently in order to perform as well as they can. Making the most of their employees is key to this success, which includes recognising that people have a life outside of the office.

I had an opportunity to lead an office move project in 2012. It was only a 20-mile move, but the business faced losing 50% of its people because they weren't prepared to relocate. I led a significant cultural change which demolished the nine to five culture and introduced agile working. This also involved creating a culture based on trust and outputs. The changes we made resulted in only 1.5% of the move employee group being made redundant.

This project made me realise that while I had been able to enjoy agile working for many years, other organisations hadn't yet embraced this approach. Implementing it within these organisations would have huge benefits for them. Having gone on to lead this initiative globally for the company I was working for, when I knew I was leaving, I realised that I wanted to help other businesses change the way they worked for the better.

Being made redundant was a great catalyst event and provided me with an opportunity to consider my next career move. I had wanted to have my own business for years, but having a financial cushion and security, I hadn't made the move. I'm the main earner in our family, so maintaining the financial income was important. That shackle was effectively removed when I was made redundant and I had time to see whether I could make a business successful.

I started to network and speak to contacts about my forthcoming departure before I left my role. I was fortunate to have several influential contacts who really felt I could be successful on my own, and they were a huge help. I was also provided with access to an outplacement programme and a coach who helped me talk through what setting up my own business would entail. My redundancy payment enabled me to consider setting up my own business while ensuring the financial security of my family.

My first consultancy assignment was offered to me five weeks after I had been made redundant through a contact recommending me to their client. That was followed by other referrals and recommendations by other contacts. To date, all of my work has come from word-of-mouth recommendation, and although this has been consistent, I have (finally) committed to a website, which goes live in June 2018, as I am keen to grow my business.

After the first year – and believing I had just been lucky with work coming to me – I decided I needed to focus on how I could develop myself and my business. I wanted to step away from the belief that I could always get a 'real job' if it didn't work out. My biggest challenge was me – my own self-confidence and belief that I could do this. The easy option would have been to stay within my comfort zone in full-time employment, but every time I considered this, another client would appear and I would continue on the consultancy journey.

I have always taken the view that running my own business should be an exciting journey and to enjoy every step, however uncomfortable they may be. And some steps have been way out of my comfort zone. I needed to be brave enough to believe in myself and open to asking for help as I had no understanding of how to set up a business. Understanding how to set up and run a business was a huge learning curve, but the help from my support network made this so much easier.

I would say to anyone considering doing something similar to believe in yourself and try. If you have a dream, make it your goal to make it a reality. I made a number of excuses why I couldn't set my own business up, but actually the biggest hurdle was me and my mindset.

Ensure you have a good support network – life as a business owner and entrepreneur is so different from being an employee. It's liberating, but it can also feel over-whelming and a little scary at times. Communicate with your immediate family so they understand what you want to do and then they can be there for you. Whether your goal is to have your own business or just change how you work within your corporate life, do your research, be prepared to take a risk, be brave, ask (you don't get if you don't ask) and give it your best effort.

Liese Lord, Managing Director, The Lightbulb Tree

Liese was able to use redundancy as an opportunity to do something different with the way she works, and she couldn't be happier. Maybe this resonates with you, or maybe you can relate to another of my clients, Kelly.

STEPPING AWAY FROM BURNOUT

Kelly came close to burnout and used this experience as a way to re-evaluate what she did, retrain and create her own business. Here is her story in her own words.

> I previously worked in corporate communications for over fifteen years before I left this career to start my own coaching business.
>
> Coming to the brink of a burnout, I hadn't been sleeping well for a long time. In the nights before I had work it was not unusual for me to sleep for only three to four hours, I was sick more often than not, I was feeling unfocused all the time and had lost all confidence in my abilities. After trying to manage this on my own for months, I decided that I simply needed help and found a wonderful therapist. I took two weeks off work (in hindsight, it was a little too short a time). I had no idea how ill I was getting, but my therapist assured me that we managed to catch my situation just before it descended into a full burnout, which would have been a lot more difficult to recover from.

With the help of months of therapy, I managed to pull myself away from burnout and develop strategies to prevent myself getting to the brink again. I also decided to share what had happened openly with colleagues, and was so relieved to receive much empathy and care. At the same time, I was also unnerved and sad to hear how many other people had suffered through something similar.

My therapist helped me to see with absolute clarity that the work I was doing and the environment I was in were completely misaligned with my values, strengths, interests and personality. In fact, at work my strengths were often criticised. Some of the warning signs were strong feelings that I didn't bring value to my work and that it brought me absolutely nothing – it simply took way too much away from me. I also felt completely uncomfortable and alien in my work environment.

During this time, I spent many hours researching other careers that could be a better fit for me. Having completed a first coaching qualification a few years before, I knew that coaching felt natural to me, so my research was mostly looking into certifications and further education in this field. A wonderful colleague had just finished her coaching training and highly recommended her school, so I signed up and got started straight away.

I started my coaching certification while still at work and transitioned from corporate communications into human resources. There I was able to gain experience in diversity and inclusion topics, which I found extremely fulfilling, and as an in-house career coach. I saved some money during this time so that after I quit, I had a small nest egg to help me with my business set-up costs.

I strongly believe in following your heart and having support to make your decisions. Leaving a long-standing career is very hard – I left communications a year after I finished my Communications Master. And you may experience resistance or negativity from others who don't understand what you are trying to do, so support is crucial to help to keep you on your path to fulfilling work. I wish I had sought help much earlier, but I used to feel uncomfortable asking for help. I don't hesitate any more; I see now that this is what made the difference.

I also wish I had had a clearer perspective, more of a helicopter view, to see what was most important to me: my health and my family, not a job that I could not stand and an income that was providing material comforts. I was so caught up in doing the 'right' thing, being a good employee and moving up the ladder in my long-standing career, that it completely clouded my view of what really matters.

A huge learning from my situation is that not all jobs are suited to everyone. My husband shared an analogy with me at the time, saying that although a rabbit would thrive in a running race, it would never beat a fish in the water. I was the rabbit in the water – I had no chance of thriving in my work environment.

My mission now is to connect my clients back to who they truly are and support them to find jobs and work environments that are aligned with their personalities, strengths, values and interests. I use psychometric assessments and coaching to help them and support them to thrive at work. I've also started an MSc in Applied Positive Psychology and Coaching Psychology to help my clients integrate the latest evidence-based wellbeing practices to manage their feelings and stress.

Kelly Campino, Career and Leadership Coach

LIVE FOR THE PRESENT

You don't need to have been close to burnout to make the change, but often big changes have some sort of catalyst; something to make you think that enough is enough. For me, it was missing my daughter's first birthday. This was the final straw. You may have picked up this book because the question 'Is this really it?' was becoming louder and louder in your head until you got to the stage where you had to listen to it. The fear of not doing has become stronger than the fear of doing.

People often ask me why I didn't change my career earlier as it was clear to them from speaking to me that I wasn't happy, but when I was in the middle of the day to day of work, it felt like the easy option to stay. I convinced myself that it would get better and I lacked confidence to take a big leap.

When some people finally make the change, they feel bad because they stayed with the same job and the same general malaise for years. I will be honest, we can all think this, but it does us no good. This book isn't about spending time feeling bad about what we haven't done; it is about focusing on what we can do next, creating a new reality where we are going to be successful and fulfilled. The past is the past, and just like future tripping, if we spend too much time there, we aren't helping our present, our reality. Whatever you have or haven't done, make peace with it and commit to moving forward.

ALLOW YOURSELF TO DREAM

The concept of opportunity cost is well known in economics. For example, I chose to go to Australia while I was writing this book and attend a two-day conference with my coach. I could have spent my time (and money) doing all manner of things, but I decided to do this. The opportunity cost of my trip to Australia and the conference was the value of everything else that I didn't do. Whatever you choose to focus on now will mean that you have to give up other things. The question for you to answer is, 'Is it worth it?'

'Judge the value of what you have by what
you had to give up to get it.'
   Tim Harford, The Undercover Economist

We are often stuck in our current reality. So many of
my team used to say they wanted to leave teaching
and do something different, but they were convinced
that they couldn't do anything else. They spoke to
recruitment agencies and were told that they didn't
have the correct skills, so they skulked back to their
safe career. They were scared. Everyone seemed to
be telling them that it would be too difficult to leave,
so why would they believe any differently? The gap
between their reality and where they wanted to be
seemed too big. And there was a time when I felt
the same.

This is wrong. I have worked with hundreds of
women who run successful businesses having lever-
aged their existing skills to build them. Plus I have
worked with hundreds more who have changed the
way they work and have never looked back.

I first thought about leaving education two and a
half years into my career, but I was scared about
how people would react. I had just turned thirty and
my dad was very ill, so I attributed my feelings of
dissatisfaction to being single and the fact that I was
working somewhere where I was unhappy. This was
all true, but I was also scared.

At the time I had a flat with a sizeable mortgage. When I looked around at other possible careers, I was told I would have to start training all over again. I couldn't see how I could afford to do this and keep my flat, so I stayed. In hindsight, if I had been serious about change, I could have rented my flat out and moved home.

How often do we hear that we should be grateful because we are fine? We are functioning, we have a roof over our heads, money, food – we are lucky. Isn't it self-ish or self-indulgent to want more? Today, I give you permission to dream. Would you love to have time to go to the gym or pursue your hobbies? Is travel your thing? How about no longer having to spend every Monday morning with your head in someone's armpit on the train? You know the life you want. You can have it.

So many of my clients have stopped them-selves having their dream life, repeatedly telling themselves, 'That isn't for people like me.' And I was once one of them. My unconscious and my friends used to say, 'Why are you complaining?' According to the magazines I had grown up with, I was living the life that lots of people desired. The tick box was complete so why did I feel so empty?

Wanting more can often seem greedy, so we convince ourselves that we need to be grateful for our lot. Of course, we can count our blessings and practise gratitude, but this doesn't need to be a block to us wanting more.

You have permission to dream. You have permission to want more in your life and not feel guilty about it. You have permission to be selfish and focus on you.

Why is this so important? Many of us are paralysed by fear – we believe that we have to act in a specific way, and if we act differently, it will mean we are wrong in some way. We become driven by the word 'should' and end up with so many 'shoulds' flying round our heads that they become all consuming. Our lives are governed by rules that we place on ourselves, and often our sense of fun is completely diminished as a result. We can be living with chronic stress without realising it, often chasing the manufactured fun of alcohol, drugs, caffeine, food, even shopping to relieve our symptoms. We feel like we should settle for fine, or we wait for something or someone to save us.

> 'You need to hear this loud and clear: "No one is coming." It is up to you.'
> Mel Robbins

You have the power to change the way that you work.

EXPLORE YOUR WHY

I want you to step away from a life of 'shoulds' and instead consider a life of 'coulds', a life of possibility. This is the time to be honest with yourself – tell the voice in your head to take a hike and explore what you really want. Today, I want you to reflect on why change is so important for you. What is driving you to create a new reality or a new way of being? Why is it important that you change now?

When you know why you are doing something, it can be an incredibly powerful motivator when things get difficult and you can't see the wood for the trees. Understanding your true reasons will help you get to where you want to be, so write down your why and connect with it. Revisit it when things get tough.

> 'Very few people or companies can clearly articulate WHY they do WHAT they do. By WHY I mean your purpose, cause or belief.'
> **Simon Sinek**

Before you read the next chapter, I would like you to complete the 'Be, Do, Have' activity (www.ruthkud zicoaching.com/membersarea/bedohave)

On a piece of paper rule three columns with the headers – Be, Do and Have. For each column write down everything that comes to mind, everything you want to be, everything you want you want to do and everything you want to have. Don't think too much about the activity and if you feel any resistance to anything move past it and write it down anyway. When you have the completed list go through it and think about why these are important to you. This will enable you to cut down the list to the core things that you desire in your life.

This activity will help you to focus on what it is that you want and identify what motivates you and why you are committed to making a change now. It will then guide you to take the action towards your goals. You can use this as a template for the next chapter and the rest of the book.

CHAPTER THREE

YOUR VISION

This is where we are going to get specific about what you want your life to look like.

Be honest, when was the last time you considered what you really desire? When was the last time you looked into yourself and thought about who you are, who you want to be, and the life you want to be living? I know that for many people, it was a long time ago.

In coaching speak, we call this exercise 'visualisation'. I would love you to think about what your dream life would look like. Take some time on your own in a space where you won't be disturbed and focus.

It can be pretty hard without prompts, can't it?

JOURNAL YOUR WAY TO YOUR DREAM LIFE

How many times do you feel like your dream life couldn't possibly work out for you? I understand; I was there too. I spent years telling myself that the life I live now was not a possibility for me. So let's consider an exercise, a favourite of one of the biggest names in self-development, Tony Robbins.

Imagine that you are retired. You are eighty years old and you have lived the life that you always wanted to live. You are sitting on the veranda of a beautiful cottage by the sea in a rocking chair and you are looking back over your life. What do you want to be thinking? Feeling? Seeing? You hear voices – whose are they? Who do you want to have around you?

Shut your eyes and imagine that you are there. Write it down, ideally in a journal especially for this purpose.

How did that feel? Now how about practising this visualisation every single day to program your unconscious mind to believe that you can have what you desire.

This is where I suggest a new habit. Journaling is what I would have referred to as diary writing when I was growing up: the process of writing down your thoughts, feelings and ideas in a reflective way. I would recommend that you spend some time each day journaling, describing your experiences and what has come up for you. You want to have clarity on exactly what is important to you and why it is important.

LIMITING BELIEFS

Many of us stay where we are out of fear – fear that if we change and challenge the status quo, we may end up even more disappointed than we are now. We are trapped in our 'fine' existence by ourselves and the barriers that we put in our heads which stop us doing what we really want to do. But we have the power to change this. We are strong and capable, and we can overcome the beliefs that we have built around ourselves.

Our belief systems have been ingrained in us from an early age and they influence how we think and behave. Many of us fear what people will say about us if we do something different. Even though we are not content or happy with our lives, we stay where we are because change is difficult. Change means that we need to act, which takes us out of our comfort zones. We fear rejection and voices saying, 'I told you so'.

This can be a scary place to be. We feel alone and we don't realise what is going on for us. But the only reason it is scary is because we don't know any differently. To make a change, we will be stepping from the known, our current reality, into the unknown. And this can be terrifying.

The comfort of the illusion of safety, of being OK where you are, can have a massive impact on how you behave. But I am telling you that not only can you shed the duvet that you have around you and take action, you are brave enough to do it now, today. Seek out the life that will give you pleasure and fulfilment. One of the biggest clichés is that life is short, and you will regret what you didn't do rather than what you did do.

Yet there is always the risk that you will end up standing on the sidelines, worried and anxious, listening to the voices in your head (they never go away; we just have to learn to ignore them). Fear of failure has really held me back in the past, even though I regularly spoke to hundreds of women who felt the same way. But I now view failure as learning, and would encourage you to do the same.

I was talking to one of my old coaches about how we need to test any strategy in business. It could be a new way of creating content, of advertising, or of running client sessions, but the premise is always the same: give it a chance and then look at the results. If it doesn't work, you will learn and will know what to do/not to do next time. We can all reframe failure as learning.

But imagine if you followed your dream and you didn't fail. Imagine if you were successful; imagine if your dream played out to be exactly as you wanted it to be. What if the vision you described in your journal became your reality? What then? What next?

Are you willing to take that chance?

Sometimes, we fear success. We worry that it will change us, especially our relationships, so we resist it. I used to worry what my husband would think if I earned more than him. I kept this fear to myself for a long time, and when we finally did discuss it, he laughed. Far from being intimidated by my success, he is happy as there is less pressure on him and we can provide more for our family. My fears were completely unfounded, and I am sure yours will be too.

If we don't have the conversation, any fears we have about how success may affect our relationships are merely hypotheses which haven't been tested. However strong your relationship, your partner/family/friends can't read your mind, so I would recommend you talk through your fears so you can make rational decisions.

PERSONALISE YOUR DREAM

One of the things I love doing with my clients is to whittle their huge vision down into something they will find a lot easier to identify with and visualise daily. Then they can start to program their brain to believe that it is possible. We can all set big goals and imagine our lives to be different, but at times this difference can seem like a chasm. We then feel over-whelmed about where to start.

From the huge vision that you created in the rocking chair test, I want you to work backwards and ask yourself, 'What does my ideal week look like? How would I spend my time?' Feel your resistance if the voice in your head starts clamouring. If it is telling you that you can't work out every day, for example, why is it telling you that? Tell your inner voice to be quiet and spend some time mapping out your ideal week. What would it mean for you to live that life? What about on a granular level? On a daily basis, what do you want to be doing?

When you do this, be honest with yourself. Remem-ber this is personal to you. Even though daily yoga and meditation work for many people, they may not for you. This is OK. As Danielle LaPorte says in *White Hot Truth*, you don't want to create another to-do list when you look at your self-care or spiritual endeavours. Do what you want to do, and when your inner voice tells you that something is not possible, ignore it and write that thing down anyway. This is about you and what you desire. Ignore any restraints, either self-imposed or from others.

Now have a look at your ideal week plan and compare it to where you are now. My client Lynsay told me that one of the things she loved most about creating her ideal weekly schedule was that she could see how everything could slot in easily. If everything doesn't fit as well in your plan or if this is completely new to you, be open minded. This is the first step. Sometimes you won't know how everything will fit into your schedule without testing it out. I remember when I started coaching and was juggling my sessions around childcare, I forgot to put any space for lunch – I only did that once!

To help you with your scheduling, and to have a look at Lynsay's schedule, click here: www.ruthkudzi.com/membersarea/schedule.

MERGING YOUR DREAM AND YOUR REALITY

What are you already doing which fits into your dream life? Most of us have some things which we want to continue doing. It may be putting your kids to bed every night, or your weekly yoga class, or date nights with your partner. You don't need to change these activities at all – as the old saying goes, don't throw the baby out with the bathwater. Remember this is your life, so keep what is working.

Now be honest, where are the gaping holes? What is the gap between where you want to be and where you currently are?

When I first did this exercise, on my list was to take my daughter to and from nursery. This was so important to me, but I wasn't able to do it, daily exercise, set time aside for reading every day, and have weekly massages and dates with my husband. All these were things that I felt would give me a better life and make me happier, so I realised I needed to make these small life events a priority rather than the bigger business things.

To begin with, my reality was a long way from my dream, but slowly the two started to merge. I used to work in my business in the evenings, and now I have transitioned across to having one evening a week for calls and working three and a half days on my business, leaving me with more free time than I could ever have imagined.

Did this happen overnight? Of course not, but setting down the intention and doing the work to get there made me focus on what was important to me. Now if I find myself working for longer than the allocated time, I always make sure I balance this with time off as I understand the importance of looking after my own wellbeing as a priority.

A lot of my clients struggle with this activity, especially if they are working in full-time jobs. Is it really possible to transition from five days a week in the office to doing yoga twice a week at lunchtime and having regular dates with your partner? If you are feeling resistance when writing down your ideal week, identify what the voice in your head is saying to you. How much do you believe it is possible to live a life like this?

This is about what is important to you. By getting clarity on what you want, you are much more likely to get there.

It often helps to look at examples of women who have achieved their ideal lives in order to understand what is possible. Women like Kerry, who balances her role as a partner in a law firm with her work for the Happy Lawyers, or Isabel who works four days a week, or Jessica (who helped me write this book) who can pick her son up from school every day. These women didn't want anything out of the ordinary and they made it happen. You can too.

GET CREATIVE AND GO PUBLIC

Another useful activity is to go public with your vision. Talk about your vision on Facebook – sharing what you want to achieve means you are more likely to get there.

Next, get creative. I am old-school, which involves cutting up magazines to create a physical image board, but some of my clients have elaborate Pinterest boards, wallpaper on their phones and on their laptops, or audio recordings of their vision so they can remind themselves of it daily. You can use anything that suits you: images, pictures, vision boards, Post-it notes or calendar alerts to keep you focused and remind you of the bigger picture. If you have a constant reminder of exactly where you are heading, you program your brain for success. Some people may look at this as setting their intentions to the universe; I prefer to regard it as being honest with myself about what I want and what gives me pleasure.

Be clear on your non-negotiables. What do you need to have in place to feel happy, fulfilled and success-ful? Be honest with yourself about what these are. It doesn't matter if your vision is completely different to someone else's as it is all about what is going to work for you. My coach made it clear she must have thirteen weeks' holiday a year to spend with her son, and this taught me a huge amount about boundaries.

Watch the bonus videos in the members' area www.ruthkudzi.com/membersarea/vision for some examples of other people's visions and how they have made them a reality.

BELIEVE IN YOUR VISION

Even if your vision feels huge at the moment, you can achieve it. When I started my business, my goal was to replace my salary and leave my job. Part of me also wanted a six-figure business, but this seemed like so far from where I was that I only had a small amount of self-belief. Gradually, with daily action, I started to believe more. Success breeds success, which is why it is important to celebrate even the smallest wins as you take action every day to move towards your goal.

Remind yourself what your overarching goal is. What is that one thing that is going to help you achieve the vision you have created? Understanding your big picture goal will keep you motivated and will be a clear way to identify where you are going. Having this goal and reflecting on it daily will help you to start taking action and setting smaller goals that are congruent with it.

'To begin with the end in mind means you start with a clear idea of your destination.'
Stephen Covey, *The 7 Habits of Highly Effective People*

The key to all of this is having clarity on what you want and understanding why it is important to you. What will achieving your goal or vision mean to you? How will that change how you feel and behave? What impact will it have on you and others? By focusing on the why, you are able to keep yourself motivated. By having clear goals, you can stay aligned – if something doesn't fit with your goal, you can make the choice to say no, which is empowering.

By now, you will likely have an idea about what you want your life to look like in terms of the big picture as well as the day to day. Are you feeling excited?

CHAPTER FOUR

WHAT ARE YOU GOOD AT?

What the hell do you do next? You did what you were told at school and you now have your career. I understand. It is fine and you are OK. In fact, other people probably think you are doing really well and are sorted. But *you* don't feel it. Ultimately, you are now prepared to take on your dream and go for it.

You have your lovely vision statement. You have possibly created a vision board. You know your goals and you may have started to take some action, but does it all feel a bit fluffy? A bit woolly? Are you really going to throw away the past ten, fifteen, twenty years and retrain for a completely different career? Or stay with what you are doing but move somewhere else? Or start up your own business? Maybe the thought of doing any of the above fills you with fear. Do you have to do any of these things? Maybe where you are now isn't that bad after all.

The most important thing is to do something that works for you. One of my most used phrases is that there is no cookie-cutter approach to success. There is also no cookie-cutter approach to happiness. We are all different, and that difference should be celebrated and used to our advantage.

INDIVIDUAL DIFFERENCES

One of the fundamental teachings of psychology is the concept of individual differences. If you read through psychological reports by experts who have used people in experiments, they always include the caveat that results are subject to individual differences. Humans are diverse and we react to things in different ways. We all have our own unique DNA and experiences, which means that we all have a unique skillset and repertoire of strengths, so let's focus on those.

In *The Big Leap*, Gay Hendricks talks about our zone of genius. This is an area in which we can operate where everything is easy and work doesn't seem hard, or boring or monotonous. In that sacred place, we are playing to our strengths and everything slots into place. We will be far more productive and effective if we focus on the things that are within our zone of genius – the things that we can do really well. Let's be honest, though, it is hard to live in this area the whole time.

Cooking is certainly not in my zone of genius, but I am competent enough at it to ensure that the family eats a balanced diet and we are all happy(ish) with the results. Yes, we do eat out and order takeaways a lot, and one day a personal chef may be on the agenda, but not right now. Many of us become the go-to person at work for things we don't love because we are competent. But competence is not enough. I want you to do what you love and what you excel at.

LET'S GET DOWN TO IT

What do you love doing? You don't need to think of it in a work context; think about what makes you truly happy and content. When do you feel fulfilled? What is it that lights you up and energises you? Imagine that you could do one thing day in, day out – what would you do that would never bore you? What are the things that you know you are better than others at?

It is time to blow your own trumpet. Perhaps you are the person who is always organised, or you are good at getting your point across. Maybe you think of things in a creative way, or maybe you are a great listener.

I was speaking to a friend recently and he recalled the time I told him I was coaching full time. He said that he had known I would do it, and be amazing at it, as I have always been the person helping people through their problems and finding solutions. He then got me another drink and, in his own words, 'got some coaching while I can still afford it'.

For me, helping people find their own solutions is what I love. And there are lots of similarities between what I do now and teaching or managing teams, in that I don't give people the answer. Instead, I help them find it themselves while knowing enough to guide and support them.

What do people always come to you for? Are you the party organiser or the person who helps make peace at home? At work, are you the person others turn to in a crisis? Are you an amazing salesperson who always nails the pitch? If you have something clear and concrete in mind now, focus on that. Focus on your strengths and what you are good at. This is where you want to be operating.

Still not sure? Go out and speak to people who know you well, for example work colleagues, friends, your partner or your family. What do they think you are good at? What do they come to you for help with?

Have a look at the dream life you imagined and journaled about in Chapter 3. What in it is aligned to your strengths? What is different? What do you want to do? Be honest with yourself. Even if you are a whizz with technology, you don't want to be working with it for the rest of your life if it bores you. It is about understanding what you love and what you are good at, then finding the real sweet spot of understanding whether people will pay money for your skill.

PLAY TO YOUR STRENGTHS

I would love to share a story here. When I first stepped into the online world, I was part of a great coaching programme. I was a little further down the coaching journey than most of the women in the programme, and I saw how they all started off doing one thing: resisting what they had been great at before. Often they didn't feel they were good enough, or they didn't realise that their skillset made them unique and special.

I also see this time and again with my clients. They come to me and want to do something completely different to what they have done in the past. And I was the same. I was advised to coach mums, so that was my niche for about a year. But it never really resonated with me. I am a mum, but it isn't the most important thing about me. There are lots of other things I think are more exciting and more relevant. I was playing into one part of my story and experience:

how I had lost confidence after having my daughter. However, this was only a small part of my life and how I could help people.

I had many skills in business – I had studied it from the age of sixteen and I had taught it. I had run my own businesses in the past and I had mentored people to be successful. Plus by this stage I had been in the coaching business for over a year. It was staring everyone else in the face what I should be doing, but it took me a while to get there – I thought everyone knew about financial planning and strategy. I discounted my experience and my ten+ years as a leader managing and developing teams. Instead, I was staying small and being generic. I was using my strengths, but I had forgotten to use all of the skills I had spent years building.

So many people are similar.

CASE STUDY – LUCY

Lucy is a video strategist. When we first met, our businesses looked very similar.

Lucy had spent twenty years as a journalist and in TV, working all over the world. She had even been on Air Force One. She was highly respected in her industry, but had launched a business that discounted all of her experience and instead focused on the one thing she had been doing for a year – being a mum.

Lucy is a qualified coach and one of the best listeners I have ever met, but she has so many other skills. When she realised she could use her skills from journalism and TV to help people with their online presence, her business flew. Lucy is the woman responsible for my YouTube channel, helping me produce fantastic videos for the last year. She has also trained many of my clients to be more confident on camera and to understand how to use video technology in their businesses.

Here is Lucy's story in her own words.

> After my baby's traumatic birth, it wasn't really possible for me to return to work in the field as a journalist in places like Iraq and North Korea. Even going into a newsroom was challenging, with my bladder issues. So I knew that I had to find a way to work from home, and earn money.
>
> I had always had a side hustle coaching business, but I'd lost my confidence, so I had to work on this before I was able to connect with people and start my business. I started small, talking to people in my network before marketing and expanding my services.
>
> Trust your gut, and don't get swayed by the 'sparkly' marketing campaigns. Often coaches with slick campaigns don't necessarily have any substance beneath the glossy photo shoot. It's easy to fall into their trap, but think carefully before you sign up.

You don't have to sign up immediately; the cart is always open.

It took me a good while to get clarity on my niche, and if I'm honest, I would have hired a much more business-minded advisor rather than a coach with a glossy marketing brand. It was only when I started being realistic about my market that I understood my strengths and how I could market myself effectively.

Lucy Griffiths, video strategist

YOUR UNIQUE SKILLS

I can't stress it enough: even if you hate what you currently do, don't close the door on your skills. Yes, making a huge shift between industries can be hard and scary, but you can do it.

When I went through leadership development training, we were assessed on a number of different competencies – things like resilience, self-awareness and analytical thinking – and I do the same with my high-level clients. These are generic skills that we can all develop. However, we all have natural abilities in specific areas, and these are the abilities that will help get us to our zone of genius and an effortless way of working.

Many people think of their skills as a series of tick boxes. Have they managed teams? Tick. Do they have a respectable job title? Tick. Have they hit their KPIs? Tick. But instead, take a step back and look at your skills, as this can be very empowering.

EXERCISE: RATE YOURSELF

To get more clarity on your leadership skills, complete the following activity: give yourself a ranking for each of the skills listed below. If you can, get feedback on these from people who know you well, for example, colleagues at work whom you trust.

For each competency rate yourself from 1 to 5, using the following scale:

1 = no evidence
2 = some evidence
3 = good evidence
4 = excellent evidence
5 = this competency is fully developed

Curiosity and eagerness to learn. Interacts with 'those in the know' to enhance own knowledge and skills. Committed to personal development and additional training. Looks to develop further professional expertise by building on their skills.

Personal drive. Sets challenging personal goals and aims to exceed the expectations of others. Always challenges own performance in order to improve.

Integrity. Acts on personal values at all times. Publicly admits mistakes.

Collaboration. Publicly and consistently credits others who have performed well. Creates clear goals that are shared with others. Networks both internally and externally in their organisation.

Self-awareness. Strikes a balance between confidence and modesty. Decisions are based on their understanding of their strengths and limitations. Identifies when they are triggered emotionally and manages their reactions.

Relating to others. Demonstrates understanding of others and acts accordingly. Builds positive relationships with others across diverse backgrounds. Is able to identify strengths and weaknesses based on understanding of individuals.

Inspiring others. Breaks down broad vision of the future into specific and concrete goals and plans. Communicates vision in a way that is easy to understand. Is able to provide direction and highlight priorities.

Developing others. Provides specific advice or suggestions for performance improvement. Understands colleagues' strengths and development needs. Gives clear feedback to support ongoing development.

Impact and influence. Considers impact of own action or words, and tailors approach to suit audience. Listens to others and adapts approach accordingly.

Analytical thinking. Is able to see the likely chain of events arising from actions. Analyses relationships between different aspects of a problem. Anticipates possible obstacles and thinks ahead about the implications of decisions.

Holding to account. Introduces new, different or higher standards of performance for others. Monitors progress against success criteria.

STRENGTHS

People who know you from work or personally could also complete the ranking exercise, so that you are able to get a balanced view of how people see you and how you present yourself to others. Remember that how you come across to other people may well be different to how you see yourself. You can have blind spots that are both positive and negative. My advice is to focus on the positives as these are where you want to spend your time. We can all dwell on what we can't do, but expending time and energy 'shifting the needle' will be most effective when we look at our strengths.

Remember also to beware of the persona effect. If, like I was, you are desperately trying to be someone else at work, worried that the real you won't fit in to the mould that you have created for yourself, you can get some unusual results. The DISC (dominance, influence, steadiness and compliance) personality profile is a tool that is widely used in organisations and for individuals. It is a tool that gives an understanding of people's behavioural differences. By answering a series of questions you can get a picture of your preferences and of the differences between your private, public, and perceived self. Go with what you feel and think more than listening to others, as you genuinely know yourself better than anyone else.

We all behave differently under stress and conflict. I am a leader and love paving the way and creating new projects, but when conflict arrives, I become obsessed with detail and data. Your profile may be similar. Remember that you won't be good at everything, and instead look at those areas that could point to your zone of genius.

Have a look at the Sixteen Personalities test here: www.ruthkudzi.com/isthisit/16personalities for more ideas.

THE IMPORTANCE OF A NETWORK

CASE STUDY – SOPHIE

I have a client who is amazing at bringing people

together. Sophie can quickly identify the strengths in others and has built great teams and managed projects as this is her area of expertise. However, when I first met her and asked her about her passions, she couldn't identify anything. She didn't think what she did was a skill because it came so naturally to her.

Here Sophie shares her story, which I am sure will resonate with a lot of you.

My job before I had my daughter was unpredictable and involved working long hours without much flexibility. No one in the team worked part time, which I hadn't really considered until I got pregnant. I just assumed I'd come back part time after I'd had the baby and didn't think too much more about it (it seemed like a long way off at that point).

Once I'd had my daughter, I realised that I wanted to be doing something I really loved in the time I spent away from her. In addition, I wanted the flexibility to be able to get her up in the morning and give her breakfast, be at home with her when she was ill, and take her on playdates with her friends. My old role probably wasn't going to give me what I was looking for.

However, the company was going through a reorgan-isation, and after some difficult discussions, my employers offered me voluntary redundancy. After a lot of thought, I decided not to look for a part-time job. Instead, I took the leap to working for myself to try and get the balance, flexibility and time with Eliza that I was looking for.

I had no idea how much working for myself would involve working on my mindset. Self-doubt, fear of failure and my relationship with money have all been things I've had to address and find strategies to improve. Also, I needed to find other people who worked for themselves and build myself a little team as it can be lonely working from home on my own. Sometimes I just didn't know how to move forward with something. None of my friends or family owned their own businesses, and at the beginning it felt a little isolating. After becoming part of Ruth's Facebook group, I started chatting to other mums in similar situations, and now I have a great group of friends who I can bounce work ideas off. We all share our skills and knowledge. Now I put less pressure on myself to try and do everything all at once. I only have about fifteen hours a week in which to work, but I was trying to cram a full-time job into that space. Inevitably, I was dropping balls and losing sight of why I was trying to find a new way to work. As a result of this, I recently took time out to do a vision board to put on the wall and remind me of my 'why', which has helped me a lot.

Sophie Griffiths, Mama Baby Bump

WORK IS MEANT TO BE FUN

When you are operating in your zone of genius, things will be easy. Often my clients say to me that they can't believe work is such fun. They can't believe they are being paid to do something which seems so obvious. One of my clients says that she loves coaching so much it doesn't feel like work. I feel the same. This is because we are operating in our zone of genius. The reason it is fun and easy is because it is what we are meant to be doing.

This is how work is meant to be, but so many of us have limiting beliefs which stop us from recognising that fact. Growing up, I got the impression that I either had to sell my soul and work for money, or I could do something I loved but be poor. Work was meant to be difficult if I was to be successful.

When I worked in recruitment, this mindset was alive and well. I had to put in as many hours as possible and then I would be successful. This was before social media, so most of us spent the hours from 5 to 8pm emailing friends, emailing each other, making tea, eating chocolate or smoking. Our brains were frazzled from being at our desks since 8am and we no longer had much motivation.

This experience reinforced my limiting belief: I was working hard, putting in the hours, and getting results. As we were recruitment consultants, the mornings and the evenings were key times for us. However, we could easily have had a two-hour break in the middle of the day to go to the gym, read, or do yoga, and we would have been more focused and productive as a result.

For nearly four years as a consultant, I ran, managed and coordinated projects. I kept being told I was too productive as I was doing more than the rest of the team and working shorter hours – I planned my time so I went to the gym and worked from home most Mondays, travelled outside busy commuting times as much as possible, and worked for short periods. I was successful and I got amazing results, but I felt like a fraud. It was all too easy. Because I wasn't chained to a desk or a location, I always thought I would get found out and that I wasn't doing what I 'should be', however much I was giving the work and getting excellent feedback.

When you are at work, what doesn't feel like work? What activities do you do where you can feel completely engaged and time doesn't seem important? I identified that coaching was the thing for me because when I was asking people questions and having them coming to their own conclusions, I felt energised. I looked forward to my line management meetings and my clients got results.

LEARN FROM YOUR PAST

Take some time to reflect on exactly what you enjoy. What are you good at? What are your strengths? Are there any key themes coming up for you? It can help to write down your career and education history – do you see any common themes? What was it that led you to study your chosen subjects? What parts of these still excite you or interest you?

Often we can find ourselves going back to those subjects much later. For example, I use the business and psychology I studied in the 1990s now more than ever, but it only made logical sense to do this when I wrote it down and took the time to look back.

If you are looking at your work history, are there some environments that you loved more than others? Maybe you were happiest working in a small team or on your own. Perhaps you loved roles where you had a lot of presenting or people management. Even if your jobs have all been different, think about the common threads.

'You can't connect the dots looking forward; you can only connect them looking backwards. So you have to trust that the dots will somehow connect in your future.'
Steve Jobs

Look at your past as a way of finding clues for your future. All of the people I know who are successful have built on what they have done in the past, and this is what I encourage my clients to do. Start collecting the clues and the facts – where were you most happy? Where did you flourish and feel fulfilled?

These eighteen questions can help you when you feel stuck:

1. What do people come to you for?
2. What do you enjoy doing?
3. What are you most proud of achieving?
4. When are you most confident?
5. What makes you happy?
6. What do you wish you could do more of every day?
7. When have you felt most excited about a project or job?
8. What parts of your current job do you like the most?
9. What parts of your current job do you find the easiest?
10. What was your favourite subject at school?
11. How do you relax?
12. What do you love doing in your spare time?
13. Who do you enjoy spending time with?
14. When do you feel most helpful?
15. What do you enjoy reading about?
16. What do you enjoy talking about?

17. What type of environment do you enjoy working in?
18. What do you look forward to doing?

Some of you may have felt some resistance while doing this exercise. Were there things that came up for you that made you think, '*I can't earn a living around that*'? Remember that you are the person who is most likely to get in your way, so allow yourself time to focus on you and your uniqueness.

YOUR OWN WORST ENEMY

Stepping into the thing that you really want to do can be scary as the stakes are much higher for failure. If you fail at what you really want to do, what does that mean? Is it admitting to yourself that the dreams you have had in a box for your whole life aren't going to come true? It can feel much safer not to try.

Even in jobs, we can resist putting ourselves out there for fear of failure. For years, I didn't tell my bosses that what I really wanted to do was coaching, so I got other things to focus on. I then found myself coaching in addition to my duties. I wanted to show I was good at it, but was scared I wouldn't be good enough, so was playing some weird game with myself which ultimately saw me in charge of things I didn't love (the operation of a school is never going to light me up).

Does this sound familiar? Whether you stay in your existing job or you decide to set up a business, wouldn't it be great if you could spend more time doing what you love during your work time? How would it feel on a daily basis? I know for myself personally and the people I work with that working in your zone of genius, using your strengths, will build confidence and a feeling of fulfilment. For organisations, you will add more value and be more productive. It is a no-brainer really.

I want you to shine a light on your strengths and own them. Once you know what they are and what you love doing, you can work on building them up and developing them. That is how you get to be the best that you can be, not by working on the things you are not so good at. Go all in and focus on the areas where you flourish. Get even better at them. It is what every successful person in the history of the world has done, so why do we think we are different?

Imagine that you didn't have money and you had to trade a skill. What would you do? We often discount things because we think that they are not going to be financially viable or financially successful, but this is something I advise my clients to stop doing. When you stop listening to the voices in your head that are telling you to do something or not to do something simply because of financial reward, it will make a huge difference to your creativity.

When you are clear on your skills, strengths and what you enjoy, this can have a positive impact on your confidence and help you make the right decision for you. I would recommend that you then do some research. What jobs or careers use your specific strengths or skills? Speak to people online and offline, and get a feel for what you really want to do.

CHAPTER FIVE
MINDSET

Do you know what is going to have the biggest impact on your happiness, your success?

You.

Fundamentally, our mindset is what makes us successful. I say this again and again, but I know people still fail to believe me. It is much safer to blame our lack of success on external factors – 'If only I had gone to Oxford University', 'If only I had long legs' etc. We can spend our whole lives looking back at our decisions and using them as a stick to beat ourselves with so we stay in limbo, doing f*** all. But this won't make us happy. It won't help us achieve our dreams and it won't change our lives, so please commit to stopping it right here.

I have clients who went to Oxbridge, clients with MBAs, clients who look like supermodels, and guess what – they are all the same. They still suffer from imposter syndrome and they still work on their mindset. Our mind governs our behaviour, so if we can reprogram our mind, we can be more successful and happier.

ARE YOU READY FOR CHANGE?

Carol Dweck talks about mindset in her book of the same name. If we have a growth mindset and we learn from our setbacks, we are much more likely to be successful. Every day I see people who are talented and could be brilliant, but their lack of self-belief or fear of failure stops them from taking action. I work with people on changing their mindset so that they can achieve the goals they so clearly desire. Reframing failure as learning can have a profound effect on how we feel and act.

A great litmus test I use with clients is to ask them if they are ready to change. Do they believe they can get there? A glimmer of hope, alongside rapport, is all I need to be convinced to work with someone. If there isn't the glimmer, forget it. If they don't believe that they are capable, they won't get there.

If you are reading this and you don't have any glimmer of hope, I would recommend working on yourself and committing to daily practices to improve your self-belief.

'True belonging is the spiritual practice of believing in and belonging to yourself so deeply that you can share your most authentic self with the world and find sacredness in both being a part of something and standing alone in the wilderness. True belonging doesn't require you to change who you are; it requires you to be who you are.'

Brené Brown, *Braving the Wilderness*

So what do you do if you are desperate to change but you can't take the first step? In her brilliant book *Stop Saying You're Fine*, Mel Robbins talks about the chicken and jerk responses. We either adopt the behaviour of a chicken in that we don't take action as we are scared of failure, so we avoid doing the things we really want to – Mel used the example of a woman who wanted to be an actress but had never gone to any acting classes or auditions – or we behave like a jerk. We feel so bad about ourselves for not taking action that we self-sabotage. For example, imagine someone who gets the job that they have always dreamed of and then starts an affair in the office. We subconsciously don't think we are good enough, so we behave in a way consistent with these beliefs.

Neither of these behaviours is helpful and neither will get you to where you want to be. My advice is to look out for them and stop them if you identify them.

PSYCHOLOGY

Now let's talk about psychology. My experience in psychology spans over twenty years; I studied it for my first degree and hold an MA as well as having experience teaching psychology. Psychology is the study of the brain and it explores how our minds work. Our minds dictate our behaviours and what we do. Our experiences, our genetics and our environment all influence how we think about things, which in turn dictates the way that we behave.

All of us have certain ways of thinking which don't serve us well and hold us back. This is why there is such a plethora of mindset coaches.

I have enlisted the help of the brilliant Samantha Colclough, transformational coach, clinical psychotherapist, hypnotherapist and mindfulness teacher, to explain how we can harness the power of the mind to get results and how we are able to reprogram our beliefs and thought patterns.

If you have the right mindset, all your wildest dreams are achievable and anything you want is attainable, right?

So, if you know this, why do you still struggle? Put simply, you haven't learnt how to leverage the power of your mind yet in a way that you can gain instant control, regardless of how you feel. The good news is I'm going to be sharing with you three simple steps that will quite literally change your life. But before we go any further, it's important to understand first how the mind works.

I want you to imagine that you have one brain and two minds. One mind is on your side, the other isn't. The one that's on your side will tell you, 'You can achieve great things.' It's the one that eggs you on to do the things you want to do; the one that pushes you outside of your comfort zone in the right way; the one that's cheerleading when you come up with a great business idea. This mind is what I like to call the conscious intellectual mind, also known as the humanistic, left prefrontal cortex, good guy, and angel, among other things.

You then have the polar opposite of that: the primitive subconscious mind, also known as the chimp, the petulant child, the negative committee. This mind sucks and is responsible for making you feel terrible a lot of the time. This is the mind that tells you, 'You can't do that, you're better off doing what you've always done, no one would ever listen to you, your business idea is rubbish, and there are far greater people out there who could do the job a million times better than you.'

I mean, seriously, why does this brain even exist? Believe it or not, this part of the brain is quite important. It's designed to get us out of trouble and get us out of trouble fast. Originally, it was designed to get a caveman out of trouble if he saw a bear, which would have obviously been great in those circumstances. Unfortunately for us modern-day beings, it pretty much perceives everything to be a bear and reacts in exactly the same way to an argument with your partner, financial troubles, or taking a leap into the unknown, for instance. This brain only knows how to operate from three parameters: anxiety, sadness or anger.

Anxiety increases adrenaline and cortisol levels, which help us make decisions instantly to avoid situations or run away from them. Once again, great if you run into that grizzly bear; not so great for modern-day living. Unfortunately for us, we've adapted modern-day anxiety to worry about everything and anything.

Sadness reduces the levels of serotonin, our feel-good chemical, and keeps us from doing anything. Therefore, we wouldn't move or leave our cave until the situation had changed. We've now adapted modern-day sadness to avoiding jobs, avoiding people, avoiding financial issues, in hope that the longer we stay in sadness, the quicker they will go away. I hate to be the bearer of bad news, but jobs and bills don't have legs. They won't walk away from you. They are there to stay until you face them head on.

Then we come to anger. Do you ever just flip out because you feel you can't take any more stress or pressure? You may be pleased to know it's a completely normal, primitive response. It was designed to increase our strength, once again to defend ourselves from crazy wild animals. But guess what? Getting angry in modern-day times doesn't make anything go away. Yes, it will help us to get more energy when we need it. But boy, do we get a heap of guilt once we've calmed down and we've realised just how 'cavewomen' we went on our children or partner.

So, we understand that this part of the brain is designed to keep us safe. But in a modern age, why are we still using it in its primitive form? Put simply, it's not an intellectual mind so it cannot be innovative. It's not an iPhone that has an update every so often; it's a floppy disk that is not going to change. We have to learn how to work with it, not against it.

More often than not, we will try to ignore our primitive mind, tell ourselves we are being stupid, tell it to shut up. Now I know with my children, if I tell them to be quiet when they've got a really pressing point to tell me, they will keep going or find another way to let me know something. This mind is no different. So, you have to learn how to acknowledge what it's saying so it feels heard, then make the decision not to take action on the advice it's given.

The other big reason that we will use this part of the brain more is down to the prolonged exposure to stress we have undergone. If you feel that you have had a 'tough' life or a not so good upbringing and have been exposed to environments, people and situations that have been less than desirable, or you've lost loved ones, gone through divorce or anything else extremely stressful in your life, unless you know how to manage that stress, the likelihood is you're very much going to be operating from the primitive mind. This mind is quicker and stronger, and if left to go feral, it will take over at any given situation.

So how do we tame this wild beast and get it under control so we are working with it rather than against it?

Step 1: Managing stress levels. The level of stress that you are currently under will determine whether you are using your intellectual conscious mind or the chimp. When you are in a place of stress, you naturally see things more negatively and have a negative internal dialogue going on, which will then become a vicious cycle. This cycle creates cortisol, which is the stress hormone, so we have to look at ways of reducing that stress.

One of the easiest ways to reduce stress is to exercise. I know, I know, I'm sure you get told this all the time, but it's true. You may be pleased to know that doesn't mean you have to smash the gym five days a week (unless you want to, of course). Any exercise that is positive and done for around twenty minutes a day will have a huge effect on reducing the cortisol levels. So, whether it's going for a nice walk, riding a bike, doing an exercise video or a stint of yoga in the morning, as long as it's positive, it will make a huge difference.

Another great way which is scientifically proven to reduce stress is to sleep. When we have good quality sleep, we enter into REM (rapid eye movement). This is the part of sleep where our minds problem solve and reduce our stresses. Now, when we are in our intellectual mind and we sleep, we are reducing our stress to a nice, healthy level. When we are in our primitive mind, any stress we've been able to get rid of, we've topped right back up again with our negative thinking. So, we then have to look at other ways in which we can replicate that state of sleep to reduce stress. This is extremely useful for mums who do not get the quality of sleep they need.

A good way to replicate REM is by using hypnosis recordings and meditation. These can be used at any point during the day, but the most effective time is at night before you go to bed, as you're putting your mind into a positive state before it goes to work.

Tip: your negative committee will try and talk you out of doing this. Remember, it is designed to keep you doing what you've always done as it's kept you safe. But we understand this is no longer useful if we are to grow and become spectacular human beings.

Which leads me on to my next point.

Step 2: Listen to your chimp/inner child/negative committee. It's trying to tell you something important and it will not rest until it's been heard. Trying to switch this internal dialogue off will only make things worse. You have to start working as a team.

That does not mean listening to what it says and agreeing. No, no, no. It means listening to what it's saying, understanding that it's only saying these things to try and keep you safe, but taking the conscious, intellectual control to move forward anyway as you have the ability to see the larger picture and the benefits that can come from making new decisions. The primitive mind cannot do this.

Tip: get it onside by giving the chimp a banana; don't lock it in a box. In other words, say, 'It's OK, I understand why you're scared. Thank you for looking out for me, but seriously, I've got this. We'll be OK.'

Step 3: Take control of your conscious, logical mind and take action. The only way you are ever going to be able to move forward and change your life is to take consistent action every day, regardless of whether your primitive mind is trying to stop you or not. It's always going to be there doing that, so get used to it. But now learn to move past it and do things anyway.

In any situation that makes you feel uncomfortable, or pushes you outside of your comfort zone, feel the fear and do it anyway. So how do we feel the fear and do it anyway? Follow step two and then count down from five to one and take action. No matter what, take the action.

With these three simple steps, you will start to change your life and amazing things will happen. You have the control to choose how you think. You have the control as to how you choose to live your life, how far you go, what opportunities you take. Don't let something you have control of get the better of you. It's an amazing world out there and it's yours for the taking.

Samantha Colclough, Transformational Coach and Hypnotherapist

Samantha has provided a bonus MP3 for you all in the members' area here – www.ruthkudzi.com/isthisit/mp3 which I highly recommend that you listen to.

FLIP NEGATIVES INTO POSITIVES

You can change what you believe to be true in the world, as Samantha has described. You can flip negative beliefs into positive beliefs. For example, if you think you are not good enough to do something, you can change that belief into 'I am good enough' and look for evidence to support this new belief. You will then be starting to change something that has been deeply ingrained in you from an early age, so taking action to change the way you feel about yourself and your beliefs can be uncomfortable. However, it is the quickest way to make enduring changes.

Working on our mindset never ends. Things such as disappointments or external events may trigger us to revert to an old way of thinking at any time. All of this is completely normal and absolutely OK. Your job is not to eradicate negative thinking; it is to be more aware of your thoughts and what is going on for you so that you can stop yourself going into negative spirals.

The advice in this chapter is likely to be the hardest to follow as you have to take responsibility for the fact that you are the person getting in your way. This can be scary. Some of our beliefs have been with us since we were young children, so there may be all kinds of things that come up for you. If you feel distress, seek professional advice.

I would love you to share in the Facebook group what came up for you when you were reading about mind-set and what you would still like help on. Why not commit to listening to Samantha's relaxation MP3 – how does it make you feel? What benefits have you seen after a week?

IDENTIFYING YOUR TRIGGERS

This is a great time to start tracking your thoughts and how you speak to yourself on a daily basis. What are the types of conversations that are regularly going on in your mind?

We all have an inner voice which can tend towards the critical. I always say that what we say to ourselves, we wouldn't say to our friends, and this is so true. One of my clients does a simple reframe – when the inner critic rears its head, she reframes and imagines she is speaking to her best friend. Immediately, her inner voice loses a lot of the harshness.

When you identify your thought patterns, especially negative ones, then you can start to change them. Spend seventy-two hours tracking what you are thinking and triggers that make you feel awful. Every time you have a negative thought write down what it is, this can be in a journal or book (so make sure you have one with you) or you can use the notes section of your phone. Alongside the thought write down any triggers – did anything happen to you to make you feel like this? Was it an event? Situation or person? What were you doing? Focus on the thoughts that are negative or unhelpful and that impact your confidence and limit your behaviour. You want to get clarity about what causes a downward spiral for you and how you speak to yourself during these moments.

When you have completed this activity, have a look for your common negative thought patterns.

Identification is the first stage of the thought process. By raising your awareness, you are more likely to know when your triggers are coming. When you're aware of your triggers, you can rationalise them: 'Ah, I am feeling like I can't do it as I have spent an hour on Instagram scrolling other people's feeds and I think they are much more glamourous than I will ever be', or 'I am struggling today as I am tired, therefore I am not going to make any big decisions'. If you can remove the triggers – for example, avoiding incessant social media scrolling or following people who make you judge yourself – then you go a long way towards limiting the impact of the thoughts.

As life coach and spiritual teacher Gabby Bernstein says, 'We have a choice when it comes to stress and negative thinking. We can proactively choose new thoughts.' She also suggests that getting rid of the negative thoughts entirely is impossible. It is more about identifying when they come up and moving on from them.

If your triggers are specific people or situations, what can you do to avoid them? Lots of my clients have made the difficult decision to stop speaking to some friends and family members. This decision is never easy or clear cut, so do what is right for you.

Personally, I don't suggest you should ever cut some-one out of your life if you don't want to, but you do have the choice about whom you spend time with and how you react to what they say and do.

If your triggers are people or situations at work, then think what you can do to minimise their impact beforehand. Setting the intention for the interaction and rewarding yourself afterwards can be ways to reduce the impact of the situation.

Understanding that you have a choice in how you feel and think is essential if you want to move forward, so practise using your choice muscle. You can do this by saying no to things at work or in your personal life which are not aligned with your goals or doing more things that make you feel better. When you increase your self-awareness, you become more in tune with your feelings and will naturally respond better in difficult situations.

Having identified your thought processes and trig-gers, you need to think about how you are going to move forward from them. Remember to acknowl-edge negative thoughts; they are never going to go away. As Samantha explained earlier in the chapter, they are your primitive brain's, your chimp's, way of protecting you. Everybody has these thoughts, so don't ever do yourself down for having them. You can, though, reduce their frequency and identify practical ways to move forward.

When you have identified ways to deal with your thoughts and tested out strategies that work for you, remember to check in with yourself regularly. Stress can manifest in many ways and your mission is to reduce its impact. For me, I like to tell the thoughts to go away, then I go back to gratitude in the moment, remembering at least five things I am grateful for. I also find that taking a break from the trigger activity and physically changing my state – this could be anything from doing star jumps to going out for a walk – has a positive impact.

Make a commitment to track your thoughts and test strategies to get rid of the negative ones. I have shared some of the strategies that work for me, feel free to share your own with the Facebook group here www.facebook.com/groups/isthisitRK. When you raise your self-awareness, you can start to make the positive changes which will help you transform how you think and feel about yourself.

CHAPTER SIX

REAL SUCCESS HABITS

Do you want to know why some people are successful and others aren't? It isn't a magic sauce or a superpower; it is because they commit to taking consistent action.

I talk a lot about daily action to my clients, at events, and on social media. The reason I do this is because I have seen daily action make the difference between someone being OK and being great. When you commit to doing the work and putting yourself out there, you will achieve your goals, even if there are some bumps along the way.

I was recently interviewed by someone who asked why I thought I had been so successful so quickly (trust me, it didn't seem to me to happen quickly).

My answer was that I have kept going, even when things felt stacked against me. My most successful clients are the ones who do something every day to get closer to their goals.

This doesn't mean that you need to be working for hours every day on your new career plan, but you do need clarity on exactly what you want to be striving for. Go back to your vision and imagine what the necessary daily actions are going to mean. It could be taking on a new project at work that will demonstrate some of the softer skills you love and want to build on, speaking to someone who is currently doing what you want to do, or sending out an email to a prospective client.

CONSISTENT ACTION

'If you're not growing, you're dying.'
    Tony Robbins

If we aren't doing anything about our dreams, they will stay as dreams. Action is the main way that we get to where we want to be, because without action, we stay in the same place. It sounds simple and it is. You can ask the universe for everything you want, but if you don't back it up with positive action, it is unlikely to work out for you.

Daily action is the first success habit that I want you to include in your routine. I recommend that you do something every day (including the weekend), even if it is only reading a book by someone you admire (Arianna Huffington, Sheryl Sandberg, Brené Brown, Mel Robbins and Shaa Wasmund have all written epic books and are people I personally look up to), or spending some time on LinkedIn updating your profile. The actions don't need to be huge; they can be bite-size chunks which slot into your days.

A great way to decide on your daily actions is to look at the vision that you created in Chapter 3 and formulate a plan based on it. Look at the ninety-day planning training here www.ruthkudzi.com/isthisit/ 90dayplans and develop your plan. I love ninety-day plans and used to use them with my teams in education. Three months is a good period of time to assess whether a project is going to be viable. It gives you time to design and embed systems, and then review their success.

In my planning training, I talk about the big rocks. These are the goals you set for yourself that are essential for moving you forward and are the perfect place to start.

However, having a ninety-day plan can be scary, as this is where the reality of your dream starts to kick in. Remember, you can adapt your plan. When you are working out what you want to achieve over the next ninety days, think about how much time you have to work on it and be realistic. If you can only give three to four hours a week, your plan may take longer than three months – this doesn't matter. As long as you start, you will get there.

ACCOUNTABILITY

If you are going through your journey on your own, it can be pretty lonely, and sometimes it is hard to stay accountable. This is your career, your job, your business, and you are in charge of your results. Your boss probably doesn't care if you get a promotion, and they certainly don't care if you start up your own business. This is why accountability is so crucial.

Accountability means having someone to check in with you that you are doing what you said you would be doing. This can be a coach/mentor or a friend. And accountability is the second success habit I recommend as it helps to keep you focused.

For this book, I would have spent years rather than months writing it without my coach's help. She is why I am currently sitting in my hairdresser's, working on draft number five (there are probably many more to come). Not only have I paid her money, more importantly I have agreed deadlines with her, and I always meet my deadlines.

Lots of my clients say that the day they are scheduled to speak to me, whether it be every week, fortnight, or month, is their most productive day. This isn't because I am going to shout at them for not achieving their goals; it is because they have made a psychological commitment to do something and they want to stick to it.

Even sharing your goals publicly in the Facebook group www.facebook.com/groups/isthisitRK will make you more accountable and more likely to achieve them, so if you haven't already done so, why not go ahead and do it now? You may even decide to ask someone in the group to check in with you to see how you are getting on. We celebrate our successes every Friday in the group and share what we are working on every Monday, so you have a built-in place to be accountable.

ROUTINES

The third success habit is morning routines. There have been heaps of books written about morning routines, and I am sure that I am not the only one who has turned up my nose at waking at five to go to the gym. That is for other people – I have two kids and one of them is not the best sleeper (although I am hoping by the time you read this that she will be sleeping through the night).

However, one of the things that has changed my business and my productivity is having a morning routine. Despite my best efforts, my routine sometimes doesn't work – if one of my kids has been up all night, I am kind to myself. I believe that we need to adjust to what is going on in our lives rather than beat ourselves up if we don't always achieve all we set out to do.

I was first introduced to morning routines by the brilliant Brendon Burchard in 2016 and have since read *The Miracle Morning* by Hal Elrod and worked with my own high-performance coach. It was about working out what was going to fit in with me. For me, that is exercise (sometimes the gym, sometimes running round the park next to my house, sometimes some gentle stretching), a large drink of water, followed by three minutes going over my schedule for the day, and then doing something creative like writing or content creation.

There are plenty of other great activities you can include – journaling, affirmations, meditation. My advice is to do what works for you and experiment. I have found that journaling is something that I prefer to do in the evening as it gets everything out of my brain so I can sleep better, and meditation also helps me sleep, although I sometimes do it in the day, too. As I am writing this, I realise I haven't done any affirmations for a few months, so I may bring them back into my morning routine. I have found them valuable in the past.

To find out more about the different types of routines, have look in the members' area here www.ruthkudzi. com/isthisit/routines.

Of course, a great morning routine follows on from a great evening routine. One of Brendon's high-performance habits is to sleep well, and I know personally I am most productive when I have had eight hours of sleep. This means being strict about bed times, getting rid of electronics at least one hour before bed, and having wind down activities so I am relaxed. I love to read, have baths, speak to my husband, even have sex pre-bed.

Work out what is going to work for you and give yourself that bedtime. Again, you may not always stick to this if you are out for dinner or drinks. If you are serious about forming a new habit and building new neural pathways, it takes twenty-one to sixty-six days to do so (like all psychology, there are huge individual differences across studies, so I recommend you aim for sixty-six days or two months to embed a new habit).

My advice is to do your best, have a goal, get support, and reflect on what works and doesn't work for you. If you feel like a complete idiot doing affirmations and you don't connect with them, they won't have any impact on you. Likewise, if you hate exercising in the morning, don't do it. This book is about giving you a toolkit that you can choose to use whenever you want. When you do things because you want to rather than because you should, you will be happier and more successful.

HOLISTIC GOAL SETTING

How successful you are in achieving your goals will be dependent on a number of factors. The great thing is you can increase your chances of success. However, many of my clients have a real fear of success. They worry that if they start up their own business or retrain, they may have less time for their family or relationship. Balance is possible, although it does take practice, so I highly recommend scheduling in all of your commitments so you know exactly how much time you have for each.

Why do I suggest holistic goal setting? This book is focused on your career, but I recommend to my clients that they set goals in eight areas of their lives:

- Relationship
- Spiritual
- Career
- Financial
- Charitable
- Family
- Social
- Health

These don't need to be huge goals like running a marathon or giving away lots to charity; they can be small. For example, one of my spiritual goals is to go to church twice a month, even though I am not that religious, as I find the experience comforting. Another is to support my husband and the family. I have weekly dates with my husband, which range from breakfast to lunch to dinner and drinks. Having these small goals helps me to stay balanced and on track in all areas of my life.

This leads me on to the next point: start with small goals and build in quick wins. If our goals are huge and far away time-wise, we often give up as we don't see the progress we have made. In terms of changing career, it can be a lengthy process and you may have lots of negative feedback, so focus on milestones that you can put into your ninety-day plan, and please remember to...

CELEBRATE YOUR SUCCESS

Celebrating success publicly gives you a buzz and helps you to build on that success. This is something I have learnt from all of my coaches and mentors, and it works. It also helps build a sense of community and social support.

How much social support you have for your goal or idea is crucial to how successful you are. By buying this book, you have unlocked access to a group of women all going through similar processes. My client Kelly describes the support of the group as being key to her success.

'Finding and being part of a community of like-minded business owners really is so supportive when you're starting out and working alone.'

SELF-CARE

Self-care is regarded as a buzz phrase that many people sneer at. However, I am a huge fan.

When I started to prioritise myself and my needs, I transformed other areas of my life as well. If you don't put yourself first and look after yourself, everything else is going to be a lot more difficult – your career, your relationships, your friendships. As you are reading this book, I'm guessing you want to feel more fulfilled and happier. One of the ways that you can feel happier is by spending more time on you. It is time to get selfish.

Self-care basically means any activity you do which is solely focused on you. This can be anything from sitting down to a cup of tea on the sofa to having a hot bath, taking a yoga class, enjoying a facial or a blow dry at your favourite salon, going shopping, going running... the list goes on. Building in daily acts of self-care – things that you enjoy and make you feel happy and cherished – positively impacts your mindset and your creativity.

You can regard self-care as small acts of self-love. Imagine you are in a relationship with yourself, and treat yourself the way that you want to be treated. By improving your relationship with yourself through the way that you talk to yourself and behave towards yourself, you are going to make a huge impact on the way that you feel. Remember all of the skills and strengths you highlighted in the last chapter and celebrate them. You are unique and you are awesome.

EXERCISE AND NUTRITION

The relationship between diet, exercise and how you feel is well documented. Earlier this year, I was feeling sluggish and lacking energy. I knew that my diet wasn't up to scratch, so I saw a nutritionist. She made me realise that I had spent years following other people's diet advice, which had left my body confused and me going through energy peaks and troughs. Now I know how to eat for my own blood sugar (and body), and combine this with daily exercise. I may not be a supermodel, but I am healthy and have plenty of energy. Plus, I feel good about myself, which is always a bonus.

My brilliant friend Gillian Kennedy is a health coach. This is what she suggests:

I work with entrepreneurs and busy, driven, successful women and men to keep them performing at their best, physically and mentally.

As an entrepreneur, your health is just as important, or even more important, than your business. Without your health, there will be no business. Eating a balanced, nutritious wholefood diet and keeping up regular activity or exercise is essential to performing at your best. It gives you the energy you need to power through the day and be as motivated and productive as possible.

It's essential that we're ultra-productive and self-motivated as entrepreneurs, as we are always juggling a million things and rarely find ourselves with nothing to do. If we're relying on sugar and caffeine and processed foods to get us through the day, we'll have massive energy slumps as well as brain fog, which will make it hard to put forward the best version of ourselves and our best work. We'll end up burning out, or worse, we will start to manifest imbalances in the body which could lead to more serious illness down the road.

Food doesn't just help provide physical energy, but also brain power. When we're eating a varied nutrient-dense diet and cutting out the crap, then we're giving our brain the nutrients it needs to do all the functions we require of it optimally, as well as balance our mood. We feel more alert, have improved focus, have way more mental clarity, and can make decisions much more easily, as well as being able to deal with stress and difficult situations better.

Exercise gives us physical and mental energy, reduces stress, keeps us healthy, and helps to improve our mental state, leading to better focus and sharpness. Especially if we're sitting at a laptop or computer most of the day, we need to be active to stimulate our circulation, our lymphatic system, to remove toxins from our body and promote a healthy digestive system. Deep breathing is a fantastic tool for coping better and dealing with stress, and should therefore be incorporated into our daily life.

Gillian Kennedy, Health Coach and Yoga Teacher

GRATITUDE AND JOURNALING

The final success habit I recommend is to practise gratitude. In the busy world we live in, we all have a lot on our plates. By making the brave decision to change careers, change the way that we work or start up a business, we are going to have some setbacks. This is completely normal. One way to stay in a positive mindset is to focus on what we have achieved and to practise daily gratitude, remembering all of the good things that have happened, however small.

On a practical level, you can do this by writing down at least five things that you are grateful for every single day. I find that it works well for me to do this in the evening as then I go to bed celebrating the day. These five things don't need to be huge; they could be eating the perfect avocado; ticking off something from your to-do list; having a lovely meal.

When you have written the list, you can reflect back on what you have written. This is another great technique for stopping negative thought spirals. Take a minute and reflect on what you are grateful for. It is effective enough to switch that negativity off.

I would love you to post in the Facebook group every Friday to share all that you have been grateful for over the last week. Sharing your gratitude publicly helps to build your positive mindset and lay the foundations for success.

CHAPTER SEVEN

TIME

The two biggest reasons why people don't change are time and money. Time and time again, I speak to people who complain about these two factors.

It infuriates me when people say, 'I haven't got time.' Why? Because they have actually got time, but they aren't using it wisely. They will use the excuse of not having enough time as a reason for not exercising, then manage to watch three hours of TV a day. If they really want something, they will make time. The old adage says that if you want something done, ask a busy person, and I think that is true.

We all have the same amount of hours in the week. It is how we prioritise our tasks and choose to spend our time that is important – remember the concept of opportunity cost? Someone summed it up perfectly on the Facebook group recently when she said, 'We have as many hours in our day as Beyoncé.'

My challenge to you is to find one hour a day that you can allocate to the new you. This may mean getting up an hour earlier, it may mean a later bedtime, it may mean no TV or social media, or using your commute or lunchtime better. I have never met anyone who can't find an extra hour.

Remember I set up my business while pregnant, working full time and caring for a toddler. I was also planning a wedding and doing a postgraduate qualification at university. I am nothing special, and of course it became overwhelming at times and I made some mistakes, but it made me prioritise my time. I didn't watch TV (and I still rarely do), I saw my friends less, and I did yoga at home rather than travel to a studio.

Some people prefer scheduling their time online while others use a paper system or a physical journal. Work out what is best for you.

If you want help with scheduling your time, login to the members' area www.ruthkudzi.com/isthisit/schedule where you can access a few tools to help you, including my client Lynsay's colour-coded schedule.

TIME AUDIT

When you have allocated your time to achieving your dream, you need to do one thing and that is protect it. Make a pledge to yourself now that you will not use this time for anything else. Think about what could impact the time and what your contingency plan is. For example, if I plan to get up an hour earlier than usual to write my book but I have a terrible night with the kids, I do it later in the day. I make sure I have the flexibility in my schedule to do this while completing my book is a priority.

In the last chapter, we spoke about the importance of routines. Having some kind of routine has been shown to be beneficial to our productivity and mindset, and if we are more productive, we will have more time at the end of the day to do what we love, which is always a win–win. Although this book is focused on finding the career you love, having a balance in your life and time to do the things that you enjoy is hugely important if you want to live your best life.

I would love you to do a time audit. Look at where you spend your time – what do you want to do more of? What do you want to do less of? And what can you eliminate? Log what you are doing and be honest about what isn't working for you. I am a huge fan of making your time work better for you, so perhaps you can combine activities such as listening to a podcast with your commute, walking with the school run, or meet friends for exercise rather than coffee.

You can go one step further by using the do, delegate and discard model. This methodology is a favourite in the corporate world as well – in fact, using this could lead to a meaningful conversation with your manager about what activities allow you to add the most value and help you to reach your organisational and personal goals.

DO, DELEGATE OR DISCARD?

When you are looking at your to-do list, think about how the activities on it will help you achieve your goals and how much you need to do. My coach helped me to realise that I was doing a lot in my business, so I started to delegate, working with associate coaches on some of my programmes.

Often when you are in your zone of competence, people will ask you to do more things. If you are a traditional people pleaser, you say yes rather than offending or delegating, but if you are doing things which are not in your zone of genius or you are saying yes to things not in your remit, you are likely to feel resentment. Resentment grows, and grows and grows until you are in a position where you are disenfranchised.

Stop doing this, now. Nobody is going to thank you for doing extra work, so by saying yes to it, all you are doing is opening the floodgates to more of it. That means less time to focus on you and your goals.

SACRIFICES

We all have a set amount of time, so map it out. How much time would you like to spend on different things? How important is it to you to have that time? If you can't find time for something in your schedule, I will challenge you to think about how much you really want it. Are you happy with your life as it is? Are you fulfilled? Are you able to commit the time to make the changes that you desire?

When I started my business, I made a number of sacrifices. I stopped watching TV, I gave up on my guilty pleasures – cheap celeb magazines and the *Daily Mail* sidebar of shame – and I stopped going out so much in order to focus on what I needed to be doing.

I now have more time to see my friends, and I can't believe I ever wasted time on those magazines. Of course, I still have my flaws – social media can be a vortex I fall into, so to stop myself from wasting hours endlessly scrolling, I schedule my time on social media into my daily plan. I am intentional with what I do.

If you struggle to keep an activity within the boundaries of your schedule, make sure you do it before an important event or an appointment that you have to keep so it comes to a natural close.

In my previous life, there were two things that drained my time: emails and meetings. I had it in my head that I had to be on top of emails and would have alerts pop up on my screen, but these were a permanent distraction, and the emails were usually not that interesting.

Meetings became the bane of my life – I have actually fallen asleep in a meeting before. When you are invited to meetings, go back to the do, delegate, or discard model. If it is not worthwhile for you to be there, be honest.

There are many creative ways that you can grab more time in the day, from outsourcing your cleaning or your admin to getting up an hour earlier. I would love you to share with the Facebook group what you are going to commit to doing.

PLANNING

To help you with your time management, I have created a day scheduler for you to plan out your days which you can find here: www.ruthkudzi.com/isthisit/dayschedule. I recommend that you schedule everything – it sounds boring, but it means you will commit. Even scheduling the time that you spend with your family means that you are more likely to do it.

One thing I am not a fan of is long to-do lists. I often think that these are the root of procrastination. When you are faced with a list of thirty things, how easy is it to waste time wondering what to do first?

Instead, try these two things:

- Write out a list of everything you think you need to do, cross off what you can outsource or get someone else to do, cross off what you don't want to do, and then prioritise the rest

- Look at the ninety-day plan that you created in Chapter 6, then look at your priorities – don't ever have more than one or two priorities each day – and pop these in your daily scheduler

Having a colour-coded schedule helps you to identify when you are doing too much of one thing and achieve the elusive balance. If your schedule is all about work, what can you change or tweak? Maybe you can be creative about how you use your commute or your lunch hour.

As I said at the beginning of this chapter, we all have exactly the same amount of hours in a day. How you use them is up to you. Make a commitment to using yours productively and ditching the things that don't work for you, whatever they are. What do you currently do that is not important or urgent? How would you feel about ditching or reducing these things?

MAPPING YOUR YEAR

Many clients come to me with the preconception that changing their career or working on their business is going to take up a lot of time. They worry that they will have to sacrifice time away from things they want to do to be a success. Although you do need to be stricter about how you spend your time when you are going through a process like this, you don't need to do so at the cost of everything else. This is why having a clear schedule and structure for everything you do is important. If your social commitments and exercise are in the diary, you are much more likely to do them. Equally, if you have everything mapped out over the course of the year, you can then go back on a granular level day by day, week by week, month by month to ensure the things that are important to you happen.

A top tip my coach Taki Moore taught me is to look at the year and to map out all your holidays. Mark in who you are going away with, how long for, and where to. Do it even if you haven't booked anything yet.

Next, map out your days off and cross them off your calendar. I work on a fortnightly schedule, partly so I can have at least one full day off every two weeks to focus on what I want. This is in addition to the day off I have every week with my children, and the weekends.

If you work for someone else, this could be when you look at flexible working options. Working compressed hours is something which is becoming much more mainstream, and having a nine-day fortnight can give you more flexibility in how you spend your time outside work.

TIMESCALES

I want to be clear on timescales. Although we all have the same amount of time in a day, the time it takes to change careers or start up a new business can be significant. This is why it is important to speak to other people who have done what you want to do.

In the coaching industry, for example, people talk about overnight success, but this rarely happens. Mindset work is usually the starting point, and the whole process will be a personal journey, so don't compare yourself and your journey to anyone else. One of my favourite sayings is 'Stay in your lane'; in other words, focus on what you are doing. If you are retraining, your new career may be years away;

a job change could happen in a matter of months. Be realistic and don't expect things to change overnight. Real, enduring change doesn't happen like that.

Remember to update your ninety-day plan and use the day scheduler or a scheduling tool which works for you. Reflect in the Facebook group or in your journal on the changes that scheduling have made to your life and your business. And if you take one thing away from this chapter, please make it a commitment to stop using time as an excuse. If changing your career or having your own business is a priority, you will make time.

CHAPTER EIGHT

MONEY

The second thing people use as an excuse to avoid making a change is money. How much money is this going to cost? Can I afford it? Will I not be able to do X because of money?

Our relationship with money can be incredibly complex and we are likely to have our own set beliefs and views.

CHOICES

If you want to retrain or you are starting up your business, you will almost certainly need capital, so what can you do to raise it? You have choices. You can work full time and fund your training or your business. You can work part time or you can apply for finance. The options are out there, but you need to be in a position where you see them as options. Once again, this is about priorities. What is more important to you – being happy long term or having money short term?

So many people don't do something because money has put them in a golden cage. Their salary is £60K, £100K, £150K, so they need to stay where they are as they will never replace it. They don't want to give up on their life-style, and their beliefs around money are such that they don't believe they can be financially successful doing something different. To them, this is not a possibility.

I am going to be honest: sometimes it does take a leap of faith to change careers or do something you love. Lots of my clients start businesses on the side at first, or they retrain while working. Alternatively, some people decide to change careers and take the financial hit.

The thing is that money can be an excuse for you if you let it, but it comes back to how much you want something. I am not suggesting that you have to go out and invest in expensive training to change your career. Work out what your goal is going to look like for you and be honest about your budgeting.

BUDGETING

Working out your personal budget and what you need to pay your living expenses is an essential part of the decision-making process when you're looking to make a change. When you see the numbers in black and white, you can then use them to clarify your decisions. I highly recommend looking at what you have spent in the past on your living expenses and talking to your partner or family about how your planned change may affect your future.

When you know your personal budget, investigate any additional costs in changing your career or starting up a business. What do you need to invest in? How do other people do it? The decision about how you are going to finance your move, if it is a consideration, is down to you and your personal circumstances.

My client Sakina retrained as a hypnobirthing instructor while she was working part time. This meant she could pay for her training and her investment in coaching and herself. She had less financial pressure as a result, so she could take her time to build her business on her terms. Ruth, however, took a different approach.

CASE STUDY – RUTH

When I started my business, I used my savings and credit cards to fund my training. I then piled everything back into the business because I believed it would work. I needed to invest in myself to accelerate my learning, plus I knew that I would be able to get the money back. I front-loaded my training and coaching, and in the second year, when I was focused on my business full time, I was able to make ten times the amount of revenue that I did in the first year (which is pretty epic).

My business revenue is growing month on month, which I partly attribute to the quality of the support I have been able to invest in. Throughout the first two years of my business, I continued to pay my mortgage, childcare and living expenses. I knew that I would have to be earning at least the same as I was in my previous career to make the business work, or I would have to have a lifestyle change.

IT'S ALL ABOUT BALANCE

You can match or exceed your financial success in different ways. Decide what financial success is going to look like for you. It could mean a change in lifestyle which gives you more disposable income or allows you to spend more time on your passions.

The best way to approach money is the same as with time. Make a plan and stick to it – it isn't rocket science. Many of the women I work with think about creative ways to save money in the short term which will give them the flexibility to retrain or start their own businesses. If you are staying in your existing career or you are looking at moving industries or jobs, then you may get a pay increase.

Alternatively, if you are negotiating reduced hours, this may give you less money but more time. The balance is up to you.

Work out how much money you need now – what are you prepared to cut back on? I cut back on clothes and nights out at the start of my business. What are you prepared to invest? Many of my clients front-load their training and development and pay for it out of their personal accounts (and I do, too). This means that they can train while still earning a full-time salary.

When you understand and demystify the numbers, you can make a plan. Maybe it will be transitioning out of your current employment to have a business, or working in a portfolio career so you can follow all of your passions, or reducing the amount of hours that you work. It's entirely your choice to make.

A LAST TABOO

Money is one of the biggest excuses that comes up when people are looking for reasons not to make a change, but it is often not about the money. I have clients who have done everything that they can to work with me. Others could easily afford coaching on paper, but chose not to spend their money on it.

One of my clients, Amanda, said to me, 'When I first

started working with you, I had enough money for the first month's payment.' Within two months, she had earned the rest of the money, despite only working one day a week.

One of the last taboos surrounds money, and this perpetuates the myth about earnings. So many people I speak to think flexible work or having a business means that they will earn less than they would in full-time employment. This does not need to be the case. In fact, in the majority of cases it is not the case (especially in the long term). Most women I work with end up earning more as business owners. Why? Because they are doing something that builds on their strengths and operating in their zone of genius. Other women find ways of working that are smart financially for them and their families.

It all comes down to your beliefs around money and how you act. Do you value what you do for a job? Are you getting paid for your skills? And, let's be honest, even in this day and age, the question still has to be asked: are you getting paid as much as men for the same job?

MONEY MINDSET

What do you honestly think about money? We all have our own money blueprint or money mindset which governs the way that we feel and think about money, as well as how we behave towards it. I want you to explore your money mindset so that you understand what is going on for you.

If you were in a relationship with money, what would that relationship be like? Describe it in detail in your journal. I know mine was a pretty crap relationship. In fact, if it had been a romantic relationship, I would have demanded a divorce.

Our beliefs about money, like our beliefs around everything else, are laid down from a young age. As a child of the 1980s, I saw lots of people who once had money, lose it, and I didn't know why. Although this didn't affect my family directly, I was very aware of it, and I recently realised how much it impacted how I felt about money. I was scared about losing my money. I was terrified that when I got money, it would disappear, so I spent it as quickly as I could.

When you look at your beliefs around money, which have the most impact on your life? For example, you may believe that you aren't good with money or that you are unable to earn lots of money. You may have a scarcity mindset where you are always fearful about running out of money.

Examine your beliefs using the following prompts:

- What do you think about money?

- What do you worry about in terms of money?

- What are your biggest fears around money?

Identify what your limiting beliefs are around money. These beliefs mean that you won't act in a way that will help you to achieve your goals. They may be rooted in fear or have been embedded at a young age due to your personal experiences.

Exactly as you did with your other limiting beliefs, I then want you to flip these beliefs, changing the negatives into positives. Collect all the evidence that you can every day to support these new positive beliefs.

For example, if you think you are bad with money, change your belief to being good with money and gather evidence that supports this. This evidence can be small actions such as checking your bank account daily or keeping track of how much money you have coming in and going out, which is what I did when I was changing my own limiting belief about money. Now I check my accounts daily and know exactly how much money I have. I also cancelled direct debits for all the things I don't use, and I never get charges (which I used to get all the time).

When you have changed your beliefs, you need to work on them every day and commit to small actions to help reinforce your new beliefs.

The way that you think about money could be impacting what you are doing in terms of your career. One way to help increase your confidence around money and changing your career is to look for real-life examples of people who have done what you want to do and are financially successful. This allows you to build up a bank of evidence to prove that anything is possible for you.

For more activities on money mindset, check out the free video here www.ruthkudzi.com/isthisit/money and start tracking your money daily by creating a simple spreadsheet with how much money you have coming in and going out. This simple habit was able to transform how I felt and behaved towards money.

FEAR

We have talked about why money and time come up as excuses for avoiding making a change, but I want to get real for a moment. What do these excuses actually mean?

They are grounded in fear. Excuses simply mean that we are scared about what will happen if we change.

There are a number of classic fears that people have, so think about how each one applies to you and what you can do to reduce the fear.

One of the biggest fears is a fear of failure. We are terrified that if we try something new, we won't be successful, and it will mean that we effectively go backwards.

If you want to do something new, especially if it is something that you love doing and think you are excellent at, the fear of failure can be very strong, and it can stop you from acting. When this fear comes up, I want you to consider what is the worst thing that could happen. For most of us, this will mean going back to where we are now. Compare this to the best result – is the risk worth it?

Another fear that a lot of people feel is a fear of rejection. If we do something different, we are worried that people may laugh at us, or worse still, it may impact our relationships with those close to us.

If you feel this, talk to your partner, family and closest friends about how you are feeling and why you are doing what you want to do. Gather an army of supporters for your idea to remind you of your goal and your why.

Then there is a fear of success – now, this is a thing! The unknown is a scary place, and we can worry about what will happen if we are successful. This fear can be strongest when we are looking at our relationships. Change can be an exciting place, but it is, by its very nature, uncharted territory. We may not want to rock the boat.

Think about this fear and break it down. What is it that you are worried about? Are the people who you are close to really going to change towards you, or are you more worried about yourself changing?

Your fears can stop you meeting your goals and achieving your dreams. You have a choice, and you can confront your fears and take action regardless. Revisiting your vision and goals is a great thing to do here, getting clear on your why. Remind yourself of your why whenever you are having a wobble. Remember the rocking chair exercise in Chapter 3? Think about what it was that gave you pleasure and why you felt the way you did.

For me, a big part of my why is my family. I want to support them and spend more time with them. I also want my two daughters to see that anything is possible and that they can pursue their dreams and be happy and fulfilled in what they do.

Do you have clarity on your why? Please do share it in the Facebook group – www.facebook.com/groups/isthisitRK. When your fears and worries come up, go back to this and remind yourself why your goal is important for you.

important for you.

CHAPTER NINE

PRACTICAL SOLUTIONS

Over the next three chapters, we will explore some of the options that you can take to help clarify your thinking. I have included examples of real women talking about what they have done, along with advice on how they have done it. These women have all changed their careers, and you will be able to see how they have negotiated their way through these changes and come out the other end feeling happier and fulfilled with their goals ticked off.

Remember to stay focused on what is right for you, your skillset and your zone of genius. Check back in on your goals and consider what makes you happy. If you are making a big decision, you want to ensure it is the right one. It may be that through taking these actions, you will get clarity on what you do or don't want in your career, and it may not be what you initially expected. This is normal, so change the way that you react if you need to.

If you are going for a significant change in your career or starting your business, it takes tenacity and time to get to where you want to go. Remind yourself daily of what you are aiming for (your goals) and what it is going to feel like when you get there. Celebrate every milestone and small success so that you stay on track, and remember to get an accountability partner to check in with you if the going gets tough.

When I started up my business, I had about eighteen months to prove myself and make it work. I knew that if it wasn't financially viable in that time, I would have to go back to my job. This was based on financial projections that I had made and the fact that I started before I went on maternity leave, so I knew I had a buffer.

When your goal is a long way away, do what I suggested in Chapter 3 and break it down into smaller actions/objectives, as well as celebrating all of your successes. This will mean that you can stay motivated and measure your progress.

As we discussed in the last chapter, you need to remember your why, especially when the going gets tough. Why are you changing your career? It may be that you have been ill and you want a different pace of life, or it could be to spend more time with your family, or perhaps you have decided that it is time to put yourself first. Remind yourself of what you want to achieve and why it is important for you to do so. Your why will keep you going and on track, so hold on to it.

SAME JOB, SAME COMPANY, DIFFERENT WAY OF WORKING

One of the ways that you can move forward is by doing the same job in the same company, but in a different way. Or you can shift where you work, but stay with the same industry. This is for you if you still fundamentally love what you do, but you don't love the way that you do it. You may be working too many hours, you may be focused on tasks you aren't good at, or you may not be operating in your zone of genius or doing what you are truly passionate about.

If you want to stay in the same company but change the way that you work, either by changing your working pattern or doing a different job, the first step is to get clarity over what you want. How would you like your job/conditions to change? Maybe you want more flexible hours or to work from home. Perhaps you would like the opportunity to work in a different part of the business or use skills that you love.

Map out what you want the change to look like and think about it from a business perspective as well as a personal perspective. We are trained to think that flexible working is beneficial to the individual, but it also has massive benefits for the business – getting well-qualified staff working at a lower cost can be great for the bottom line. Often, part-time staff can be as productive as full-time staff.

CASE STUDY – ISABEL

Break down the benefits of your desired change so they are clear to see. If you have any numbers or statistics to back up your case, all the better.

This is what Consumer Insight Specialist Isabel Lydall did. She has been promoted twice in the last five years, which she managed to do around two maternity leaves. She moved to a four-day week after her first baby. This has enabled her to build her career and achieve the balance she desires.

Isabel was clear about what she wanted. She enjoyed her industry and company but wanted to work in a different area of the organisation. Equally, she wanted to protect her time with her family for one day a week. She was able to present a business case which enabled her to get what she wanted, as her employers could see the benefits to themselves as well as to Isabel.

Here is Isabel's story in her own words.

Having a family inspired me to change to a job I love, and find a way to combine a corporate career with family life.

I'd been wanting to make some changes to my career even before I had a family – I used to work in a more general marketing role but wanted to specialise in Consumer Insight and Strategy. Staying at home was never on the agenda for me, but after having my first baby, I found I wanted to make every moment away from my son count. This gave me the courage and determination to badger my employers into letting me make a sideways move into their Consumer Insight function when I came back from maternity leave.

This idea of making every moment count has inspired a few changes for me. As well as allowing me to continue to do a job I enjoy, it has meant me working much more efficiently and keeping focused on what is going to get the best results for the business with the minimum of faffing and timewasting. In my new job, this means questioning everything: clarifying exactly what people are trying to achieve and why, and saying no to, or modifying, requests more often if they don't make sense. On a selfish level, this helps with my workload, but it also helps the business as I focus on the right things, sharpening up my thinking and decision making.

I've learnt to be proactive and organised, so I can plan and don't end up with last-minute rush work. This has helped the business be more proactive as we've got ahead on some of our strategic planning. It means being resilient and not wasting time getting emotional about setbacks or changes, but I think being a mum helps loads with this as I have realised there is life outside of work.

In practical terms, a big enabler is that my partner and I share childcare and chores equally. We are lucky in that his job is quite flexible, which makes it easier, but I have a fundamental expectation of equality. I am not 'lucky he helps', as some people say. We split the children's drop-offs and pickups, and he takes more than his fair share of things like off-nursery sick days. The 'mental load' and the family admin are mine (this works as they can be fitted around working hours).

It took a while to learn what the limits of my energy are and how to prioritise so that the important things happen and we don't burn out as a family. This does mean saying no to some things – social life and exercise are less of a priority for now, but it won't be for ever.

I dropped my hours slightly to four days giving me a day each week off work. This creates enough slack in the system to do what I need to at home while still being around at work enough to be in the thick of the action. Slightly controversially, the boys are in nursery on my day off, which means chores and admin take a fraction of the time they would with little ones about, and I get a bit of time out. Then weekends are clear for spending time as a family.

I believe that it is possible to be successful in a corporate career and have a decent family life. For me, the combination of equality at home and slightly reduced/ flexible working hours makes the difference between thriving and burnout. In fact, since I've had children and been much more focused in reduced hours at work; my work has actually improved. I've become more confident, more resilient, more effective, and it's not just me saying that – I was promoted to lead my new team within a year of joining it.

On a feminist note, I don't have much time for 'mummy guilt'. So many working mums I know feel torn and that they aren't doing a good job at work or home – which is pure nonsense. How many working dads would say this, and how many would feel judged for trying to succeed at work and also be a good dad? I think it comes from how much we women can feel judged for our choices, and try to prove all our critics wrong (even the ones who don't exist). In most cases, this simply wastes emotional and mental energy that would be better put to positive use. Plus, it can make us vulnerable to other people laying on the guilt to get us to do things – both at home and at work.

It took having a family to give me the impetus to fight for the career I really wanted and make it work without working long hours. If I could advise my past self, I would have done it much sooner. Being more confident, asking for what I need, and arranging workload and home in a way that works have been easier than I thought.

Otherwise I don't think I'd do anything differently – which is not to say everything is or was perfect. But you kind of learn as you go what to do and what not to do again.

Isabel Lydall, Consumer Insight Specialist

FLEXIBLE WORKING

Think about how your proposal is going to impact the business that you work in and why it makes sense for your employers to support you. Be clear about the mutuality of the agreement.

Liese Lord, Managing Director of The Lightbulb Tree, has the following advice if you are seeking flexible working:

Asking to change the way you work can seem more daunting than it actually is. Your manager is human; they will likely want to support you and they may have concerns about the changes you are seeking.

The best flexible working arrangements tend to be those which are informally discussed and agreed. Consider this approach first – you've got nothing to lose and will always have the formal regulations to fall back on:

· Approach the subject as a two-way conversation – successful flexible working is based on trust and great communication

- Show that you have thought through the situation from your employer's perspective as well as yours

- Anticipate queries and concerns that your employer may have and think about what you could say or do to reassure them that your request will work for both sides

- Show you are truly flexible, even though you may have rigid reasons for the changes such as fixed childcare times. Acknowledge that you can be flexible when your employer needs you to be, providing you have reasonable notice. The ability to give and take will be repaid on both sides many times over

- Have a plan A, B and C. You may need to compromise slightly on your ideal, but be open to the fact there could be really good reasons for that compromise

- Do consider suggesting a trial run or pilot. Test the changes for a couple of months and see how they work for both sides. Be open to tweaking what you and your employer have agreed if it becomes obvious it's not quite right. Offering the option to test/pilot helps people embrace the changes more willingly

Liese Lord, managing director, The Lightbulb Tree

If this sounds like something that you want to do, create your proposal using the template in the members' area.

SAME JOB, DIFFERENT COMPANY OR INDUSTRY

An alternative to doing the job that you love in a different way could be moving companies. Look at the other companies in your industry and see if there are any that resonate with your values more than your current employer, then approach them. They may be looking for people with your skillset and experience, so be clear about how you can add value.

If you love your job but don't love where you work, it may be down to your colleagues, the office politics or the physical location. Write down a 'shopping list' of what you want to have in a new job and do some research into companies in your industry. It may be worthwhile to speak to recruiters, especially if you have niche skills and experience, as they can often be a valuable source of information.

Spend time researching the companies on your list, and if possible speak to other people who work for them. You can connect on LinkedIn, and consider mutual connections through your network. It may be that some roles are not advertised or don't come up that often. If you have a hit list of companies which are aligned with your values, you can apply speculatively or speak to their HR departments and ask to be informed when vacancies come up.

Moving to a new company can often be like wiping the slate clean, and is an opportunity for you to refocus on what is important to you. It can be one of the easiest ways to change your conditions, but remember to negotiate what you want at interview and be clear about your boundaries from the start.

USE YOUR SKILLS FOR A NEW JOB

This can often be one of the hardest moves to make as traditional recruitment consultants will find it tough to place you and often won't touch you unless you have direct industry experience. Do not let this put you off. Many of your skills will be transferable.

Look back at your list of skills and strengths. What makes you stand out from the crowd? What would you like to use in a new role? When you are researching new careers, always look at the job description and person specification. If you have at least 50% of the skills on the person specification and you are confident that you will be able to do everything in the job description, go for it.

When I worked in education, so many people would say they wanted to leave but they didn't feel they had the skills. They stayed as they couldn't see how they could use their skills in a different job. Often people will say they can't make a move, or if they do, they will have to start at the bottom.

CASE STUDY – JODIE

If your role has given you leadership or management experience, these can be good skills to leverage as leading and managing teams is pretty similar whatever you do. Jodie DeVito did just this. After leaving teaching and working for a local authority, she decided she wanted to get out of education so she moved to a new job where she progressed up the ladder to director level. Jodie was more successful in her new career and her financial rewards were good from the outset.

If she had listened to all of the naysayers, she wouldn't have got there. Many people tried to discourage her from making the move, and recruitment consultants would just say a blanket no when she asked about training roles or similar. Here is Jodie's story in her own words:

> I trained to be a teacher because I wanted to do something that mattered and, like many people, I feel passionately that education matters. I took a route into teaching that was real in-at-the-deep-end stuff and, although it was the most challenging few years of my life, I loved it and stuck it out through the frustrations and hardships because it was rewarding and I felt that I was living by my values, doing something worthwhile. And people kept telling me it wouldn't always be so hard... it would get easier... I would achieve

work/life balance... I wouldn't always be exhausted and broke... but... none of these things came true for me.

I was aware that I was always complaining about the workload and my issues with the system, and when that happens, you have to re-evaluate! Yes, there were many aspects of teaching that reinforced my values and gave me satisfaction, but over time, these had become overshadowed by the things that bothered me. I had a conflict and needed to ask myself the serious question: is this worth it?

In those airline safety demos that we all know by heart, they tell us to put on our own oxygen mask before trying to help others – it's a useful analogy we can apply to our lives. I'd already sacrificed and invested so much; I believed if I kept working harder, giving more, that I'd reach some point where everything suddenly fell into place. I couldn't see I was burning out and becoming negative and cynical in the process – not a great springboard for inspirational teaching and not a fun person to be around! I'd lost sight of myself.

By trying so earnestly to live by my values, I'd forgotten the most important one of all: self-care. In fact, I don't think at that stage in my life I'd really understood what self-care really means... it means put on your own oxygen mask first.

I went to my head of department and the head teacher for advice, but of course, they tried to convince me to stay because then, as now, the education system was facing a crisis of recruitment and retention. It was not in their interests to offer impartial advice and not in their power to alleviate the challenges of teaching – challenges they were dealing with themselves – so they told me it would get easier, that it would be a mistake to leave, to throw away all those years of training and experience; it would be completely nuts, they said, to start a new career outside teaching.

Well, I've always believed that 'fortune favours the bold' so I made the decision to leave anyway – I could see that the only way things were going to change was if I made that change happen.

And guess what...?

It turned out that there were a gazillion jobs out there that were begging for ex-teachers. Not only did I *not* have to abandon my training and experience – they proved to be a huge asset in other related sectors that valued my insight. In teaching, I was surrounded by other teachers who shared the same knowledge and skills; outside of teaching I was seen as a specialist!

I found a job in the publishing field – where the schools market is a cornerstone of their revenue – and to my delight realised that, outside of the public sector, hard work and results are rewarded with pay rises and promotions. And I didn't have to compromise my values, either. Because I didn't have a commercial background, my starting point was never around how to make the most money; rather, I looked for solutions to the challenges around schools funding and, through my understanding of how teaching and learning work, found ways to do deals that benefited the schools and my employers – solutions that were cost effective enough to be taken on board by the Department for Education as part of a national policy, which in the end, by virtue of economy of scale, *did* increase revenues for my organisation. Everyone's a winner!

I will never regret becoming a teacher – with all its ups and downs – but I will never regret leaving teaching, either. I needed both stages for my career to really take off. If I had resigned myself to putting up and shutting up, if I had listened to people telling me that abandoning my career was too risky, I would never have known what else was out there – and there was *so much* out there! I'm grateful I listened to that voice inside me that kept telling me what I was doing was not right for me – always listen to that voice! Your job does not define you, you can take what you learn and apply it to new areas so that you keep growing and enjoy what you do. You shouldn't feel you have to get work over with in order to resume being you – life is too precious to put on hold while you work! When you enjoy your work, it doesn't have to be sectioned off from the rest of who you are but feeds you as you feed into it.

My advice? Look after yourself – take regular time out specifically to evaluate your situation, weigh up the positives and negatives – nothing's perfect all of the time! And when the balance swings too far in the wrong direction, make a change. Don't fear change and do have faith in your ability to make change work for you. Trust your inner voice and remember that it might not shout so make a quiet to time to hear it.

I take ten minutes each morning – I call it my meditation time, which is not strictly accurate, but it's something that people understand and generally respect. In fact, it's a conversation with myself, which is why I think it's important to do it when I first wake up as there seems to be a better chance of connecting with the inner self at that time. If dreams are messages from our subconscious, it makes sense to use that channel while it's still open, before everyday life crowds in and takes over. Generally, it goes something like this:

- How do you feel? Do you know why? (I don't force the answer to the second part – like the name of the actor in that thing I can't remember, it always comes to me at some later point in the day or week, when I'm thinking of something else!)

- What's important to you? (Usually, here, I remind myself of my values and the person I want to be – it helps me to have that fresh in my mind as I go forth into my day. Sad but true!)

And that's it!

For me, the quality of my day hangs off this short, quiet time of introspection in the morning. It's very easy to put it off – it can sound silly, self-absorbed and difficult to defend, even to myself sometimes... But over time I have learned that it makes *all* the difference. Making time to listen to yourself is a crucial part of self-care – the more you listen to your inner voice, the more you'll learn to trust it; do it every day and you won't reach that oxygen mask crisis point!

Jodie DeVito, Commercial Director

As more companies become aware of flexible working and the importance of happy staff, they open up to different ways of working. Many companies in the tech field hire on skillset rather than experience.

If you love your job but not your company, then LinkedIn or recruitment agencies can be really useful. You can also make some direct speculative approaches to companies that you admire and would like to work with.

In terms of moving industry, ensure you have a skills-based CV and are able to give examples of how you do your job.

When I switched careers from recruitment to education, the two didn't seem aligned. But as a business teacher, I was able to apply all of my experience and knowledge of working in business, and this helped me to progress more quickly in my second career. I was using all of the things that I had learnt in a new way and it was clear that these were having an impact. As a senior leader in education, I was able to draw on my team-management skills and my experience in business to help the team look at things in a more commercial way.

The skills you have may not always be obviously transferable, but everything you have done will help you in your new venture.

If you are looking to stay in your current job but do it in a different way, look at the flexible working proposal in the members' area here: www.ruthkudzi.com/isthisit/flex

CHAPTER TEN

RETRAINING

One of the most common ways to change careers is by retraining to do something different. This can often be done alongside a full-time or part-time job, and some firms may even pay for you to retrain.

There are a few reasons why you may retrain. You may be looking to set up your business in the future or looking for a new employed role.

Before committing to retraining, do your research. Speak to people who have taken the route that you are looking at – what advice have they got for you? Find out about the best courses and what is going to work best for you. Are there specific accreditations for the industry you want to enter? Go to open days and find out about graduate destinations. If you can, shadow someone who is already doing the job you want by using a company such as ViewVo to see if you really love what they are doing.

Work out how you can make the time to retrain and commit to how it will look in your week. Retraining is a huge step, so you want to ensure that it is the right thing for you. Have the all-important plan in place so that you know exactly what it will mean for you in terms of commitments.

TWO REAL-LIFE EXPERIENCES

My client Sakina went from working as an actress to building her own hypnobirthing business while working part time in finance. This is Sakina's story:

> The main reason for change was needing greater flexibility to be with my children but needing to earn an income after becoming a mother.
>
> My prior career as an actress meant that work was erratic, and it wasn't easy to find childcare that was flexible and affordable to work with it. For me, I wanted to be at home more, and as a family, we felt that more stability would benefit us all. This was more from my husband's perspective, but I could see the benefits. Acting was anything but stable in terms of time and earnings, but as a contributor to the family finances,

I needed to find a way of continuing to work that would fit with my change in life.

I wanted to be around for my children and enjoy time with them while they were young, but I was also used to loving my work and finding it an enriching and nourishing experience. This was something I needed to have in my next career, even though I wasn't sure what that would be at the time I decided to make the change.

I had previously run my own agency and knew that working for myself was incredibly fulfilling and more confidence building for me than working for others. I made the change gradually, first finding a part-time job that would cover my income needs, and then saving from that to retrain as a hypnobirthing instructor. At the time of taking the part-time job, I did not know what I would do next, but I knew working in a corporate environment was not fulfilling for me. I needed an autonomous and creative outlet as well.

It was after my second birth experience that I knew I wanted to teach hypnobirthing and work with women who had previously gone through challenging and difficult births. After I trained, I had to set up a business. Working part time offered me the opportunity to do this without being utterly exhausted, but there were still challenges. Shifting my headspace between two jobs while working to establish my own business and still be a present and available mother was time consuming, and sometimes the juggle was overwhelming.

My advice is to plan ahead. I knew I wanted to grow my own business, so I would need to find capital or borrow money, and needed to know I could pay that back. Know what your financial commitments and desires are, and put the hours in during the early stages to maintain them while you get going. It gets easier over time.

Take your time. I used to see friends who didn't have to earn interim money and felt they were lucky as they had all the time in the world to work on their businesses, but that wasn't the truth. I was and still am building my business genuinely in the time that is right for me, and I am growing with my business.

Get outside help and invest in yourself. This was a big deal for me, as taking on too much in the home while working two jobs easily led me to feel exhausted and overwhelmed. Another way to avoid feeling overwhelmed is to seek guidance to go up to the next level. I started working with a coach, and this really shifted things for me and supported me in creating the business I envisaged rather than staying stuck at each internal hurdle.

If I had to do it all again, I would put my needs first more. In the early days, I felt I 'gave up' a lot for the needs of my family and lost a bit of myself in the process, but now I understand my sense of wellbeing is important to me and those around me. I would have made the transition from one career to another a little more seamless financially. Having money, some time and space to start well is very useful.

Sakina Ballard, Tranquil Birth

Gillian Kennedy changed from working as a chief stewardess on superyachts to starting her own business in health and wellness.

I've been passionate about health, fitness, nutrition and yoga for years. I'm a qualified naturopath and health coach, and I wanted to pursue my passions by working in wellness as a health and lifestyle coach. I knew after meeting the demands of billionaires in the superyacht industry for many years that I wanted to run my own business so that I could still have the location independence I'd been used to, but also the freedom to do things my way. I wanted a career in something where I could help make a difference in other people's lives and positively impact the world.

I made the change after I spent time getting my qualifications and realised that I wanted to do something that lit me up, that I was really passionate about, and that helped and empowered people to live healthier, happier lives, like I've been able to do. I also wanted to have more control over my life and where I lived rather than having to live with twenty-plus crew, and have more time to do the things I love.

The advice I would give is:

1. If it's possible, don't leave your day job until you've got clients or have started earning money in your business. If you can cut your days or hours down so you have more time to work on your business, then that is optimal.

2. Take courses that help you in all areas of your business. We are all specialists in a few areas, but there is so much more to learn about running a business – things I really had no clue I would need to know. Find a mentor or get a business coach.

3. Make as many close connections as possible with other entrepreneurs. This is a game changer. Create a mastermind group with them to help keep each other accountable and to support each other. Running your own business can get lonely at times, and these relationships are really important to feel like you're not alone. Others are going through the same.

What would I do differently if I could do it again?

Oh, many things! I definitely wouldn't assume that I could do it all alone, and I would have kept a day job while building my business to take the pressure off my passion having to earn me a living. There's enough pressure as it is in a new business – we don't need to add more.

Gillian Kennedy, Health and Lifestyle Coach, and Yoga Teacher

DUE DILIGENCE

When you retrain, you need to do your due diligence. What is it about the new role that appeals? Will it enable you to live your perfect week? Find out as much about the different options as you can before you start so that you choose what is right for you.

Equally, explore the money before you commit to training – what kind of income can you expect? How long will it take you to get there? What is the industry like?

I retrained as a teacher when I was twenty-seven and began my formal coach training at thirty-two, so I am a big fan of retraining and getting new skills. When I became a teacher, there was a clear career path. Initially when I trained as a coach, I did so to help me in my existing role (at the time I was a consultant and advisor) and because I loved it. I hadn't seen it as an end goal in itself, but knew that I wouldn't regret the training.

When you retrain, your journey to your ideal career can take more time. If this is the route for you, complete the career plan template here: www.ruthkudzi.com/isthisit/careerplan. Part of the pre-work for this template is to speak to people already in the career you are looking to move into and find out what they do. Work shadowing can also be beneficial as you want to ensure that this is the right move for you. This pre-work will help you identify the best course for you, given your circumstances.

CHAPTER ELEVEN

BUILD A BUSINESS

Perhaps your dream is to create a business based on your existing skills, just like I and lots of my clients have done. Having your own business means that you can have more control over the work that you do and how you work, which suits a lot of people.

The number of self-employed people is rising all the time, but like anything, having your own business comes with downsides. Being an entrepreneur can be tough and it takes a certain amount of resilience and tenacity. It isn't for everyone.

INDUSTRY RESEARCH

If you are starting your own business, do your industry research. There are some industries, like coaching, which have low barriers to entry (a laptop and a phone plus a Leadpages subscription), but the people who are successful in any industry are those with relevant training, experience and skills. When you are researching your industry, decide how you are going to position yourself. What is it about you that will make you stand out and be unique? If you are unsure, go back to your list of skills and strengths. These are what will make you stand out, so highlight them.

After you have researched your industry, look at your dream client. Who do you want to work with? (Your dream client is often you at some point in your life.) This will help you with understanding your target client's needs and the services that you want to provide.

Having your own business, especially one with digital products or an online presence that is scalable, is the easiest way to create a freedom-based life-style in my opinion. If it appeals to you, go to the members' area to download the business plan here: www.ruthkudzi.com/isthisit/businessplan.

PRACTICAL SUPPORT

In terms of starting a business, there may well be many ideas going through your head, so you have to consider what practical support you will need, from legal structure to accounting.

Many new business owners, like Caroline Rae, a Leadership and Career Coach, work alongside a mentor for one-to-one coaching or in a structured programme. Here is Caroline's story:

I changed from working in sales and marketing to running my own business. I had always moved jobs regularly early on in my career. It wasn't a conscious decision to do this, but I would just go with the interesting opportunities as they presented themselves. I realise now that having new challenges, building programmes and teams in new environments with new people, and constantly being able to learn, is where I flourish. Freedom is a core value of mine, and so I knew that setting up my own business was the route to achieving the variety, flexibility and growth that I love.

It wasn't terribly well planned; it was a mix of circumstance and deciding to go for it. I had been working as a freelance consultant for a number of years, usually with the security of one mid- to long-term contract at a time, and I was coming to the end of my time with my primary client. While the money was extremely good, I knew it wasn't the right work for me.

I'd been thinking about training as a coach for a while, and so I decided to take the plunge and do my coaching qualification while doing as much short-term freelance work as I could to support me. I then started working alongside my own coach to build my coaching practice. My advice? First and foremost, do the work that makes your heart sing – it can be hard work to get there, but it's beyond joyful. Second, plan out what you want to achieve and how you are going to get there. I jumped (which is my style), but I wouldn't recommend it.

If I could go back, I'd have done it sooner. I'd have got a coach sooner. I'd have invested in building up my confidence and self-belief sooner. I'd have understood what my values and strengths meant for me at work and what really drives me sooner.

Caroline Rae, Coach

A DREAM LIFE IN THE SUN

The final solution is to ditch it all and go abroad like the lovely Rachel. She set up her business and decided to live out her dream life with her gorgeous dog Rafa in Barcelona.

I often get asked why I gave up my career in advertising to do Reset Button. On paper, it was a perfect job. I got to work alongside creative, intelligent people. I went on exciting trips all over the world. It was well paid. Intense sometimes. Frustrating many times. But everything I did was in a team, so if it ended up being an all-nighter, I'd never be alone.

I'm a people person. Hard work doesn't scare me. However, after fifteen years of film shoots and recording, studio catering, late nights out with the clients and long boozy lunches, I felt like I'd lost the real me. I'd blinked and fifteen years had passed. I was unhealthy, overweight and tired all the time. Yes, I'd written ads for some of the biggest brands in the world: BMW, AT&T and the BBC, won international awards, Webbys and Cannes Lions, worked in some of the best agencies in London and New York, but it didn't make me happy. My career was booming, but something niggled me so much I eventually asked for a sabbatical.

The sabbatical gave me a chance to rid myself of all the layers of work and drama and people and commitment. Six months alone in Brazil brought me back to who I am, what things really make me happy. I began to look after myself. I was introduced to mindfulness, practised fitness and yoga, spent my time learning about nutrition and how to nourish myself properly.

By the end of the six months, I knew I couldn't go back. This was my chance to change my life. A chance to reset.

I wanted to find a way to give people the chance to experience what I'd felt in my time away, to gain the huge benefits it had given me, but in a realistic chunk of time. So I set up Reset Button. Rather than taking six months, clients can come to a standstill and rid themselves of all the layers that hold them down. Learn and educate themselves. Listen to their bodies. Nourish themselves. Then leave with the knowledge and all the tools to keep it up.

I've lost two stone since setting up Reset Button just by listening to what my body wants. I have an active social life. I still work hard and play hard. Constantly on the go. Love eating out, huge fan of Rioja. But I know my body's signs; I know my strengths and weaknesses. I keep up my mindfulness practice almost daily. It's my treat to myself. I feel healthier, more awake, more capable of doing anything than I have in all my life. Most of all, I'm happy.

I would say to everyone else, just start. Whatever it is you are thinking of doing, it's never going to end up anything like you expected. So stop faffing about and worrying about the tiniest detail. That detail is going to change anyway. Give it a go. And trust your instincts. Remember, so many people have been through where you are, and we're all still surviving. Stop the talking, the imagining, the planning, and just get doing.

Rachel Le Feuvre, Reset Button

For me, starting a business meant that I could have more control of how I worked and what I did. It matched my skillset and it was a fantastic opportunity to build something for the future.

OVER TO YOU

Now you have your solution, what are you going to do? We are on to the scary part: taking the actions you need to get you there.

Remember to revisit your ninety-day plan and create a new one each ninety days to help you stay on track with where you are going. The solution is usually found in small incremental steps that you can take every day which will get you closer to where you want to be. Commit to taking these steps and reflecting on your progress in your journal.

Regular journaling where you focus on what you have achieved can be transformational for your mindset, and it is a great place to refer back to when you are having wobbles or you are in an 'in between' stage where progress seems to be stagnant. Daily action and reflection helps you to get perspective on what you have done.

When you are finding the transition hard, revisit your vision. Go back to what you want to achieve and spend some time imagining what that would feel like. Visualising success on a granular level with as much detail as possible has been shown to result in a higher chance of reaching goals. Reconnecting with your vision can be motivating and helps you to see the bigger picture when things are hard and you are struggling.

Social support helps you with accountability and enables you to reach your goals. Connect with other successful women in the Facebook group to build your network and your social support. If you are a business owner or you are considering starting your own business, I would love to invite you into The Hub, my membership community. This provides you with accountability, training and a fantastic community of like-minded women. For details on how to sign up, check out the members' area.

To supplement the book, please login to my members' area www.ruthkudzi.com/isthisit, where there are practical tools, interviews and resources to help you on your journey. For support, you can join the free Facebook group here:
www.facebook.com/groups/isthisitRK

ACKNOWLEDGEMENTS

Jessica Killingley, for her help and support in prompting me to write the book, structure it, and get it done.

Christian Kudzi, my husband, for all of his help and support throughout writing the book and the many edits.

Shaa Wasmund, my coach and mentor, for being a continued inspiration and modelling for me how to get things done.

Noor Hibbert, my former coach and a great friend, for listening to me speak about the book on our trip to Australia and for helping me believe in myself.

Anne Barton, my leadership coach, who showed me what a great coach could be and inspired me to go down this route.

The team at Rethink, for helping me structure the book and make my manuscript into a fully-fledged book.

To all of the women who are part of this book and all of those who have supported me over the years.

ABOUT THE AUTHOR

Ruth Kudzi is a Business and Mindset coach who works with female entrepreneurs.

In writing *Is This It?* she has drawn on her experience as a recruitment consultant, deputy head teacher, and subsequently as a coach working with over a thousand clients. Her experience as a coach, leader and consultant, combined with her qualifications in psychology, coaching and business, has revealed to her that everyone faces similar challenges in finding purpose and fulfilment in their work. This prompted her to share her insights with a larger audience. She helps people to start up and scale businesses and to develop confidence, and she enjoys speaking to audiences to inspire them to create success on their own terms.

To find out more about Ruth and her work:

- Visit her website: www.ruthkudzi.com

- Join her Facebook community: www.facebook.
  com/groups/empowermentcollective

- Connect with her on LinkedIn:
  www.linkedin.com/in/ruthkudzi

Lightning Source UK Ltd.
Milton Keynes UK
UKHW04f1143260818
327819UK00007B/118/P